HORACE & DORIS

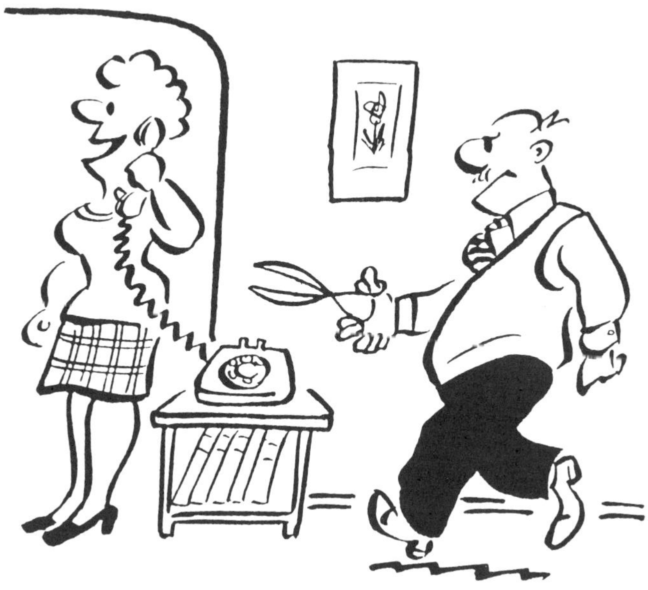

HORACE & DORIS

First published in Great Britain 1992 by
VISUAL HUMOUR
Cleveland, TS18 5LF, England

ISBN 0 9520027 0 1
Printed by Falcon Press (Stockton-on-Tees) Ltd.

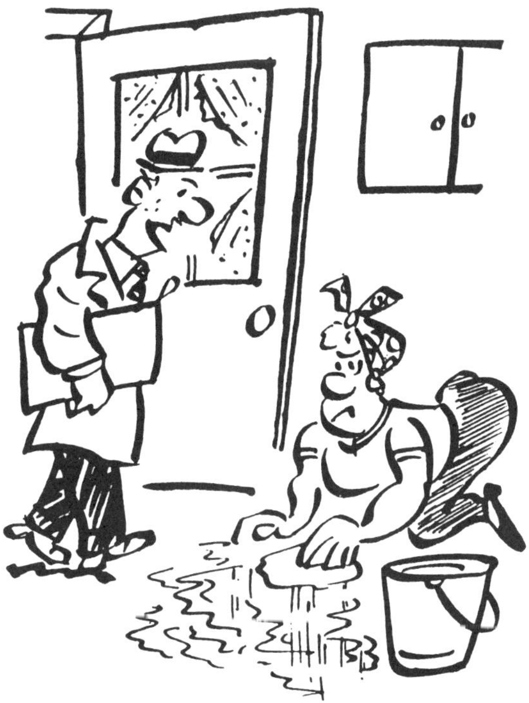

"I like your hat."

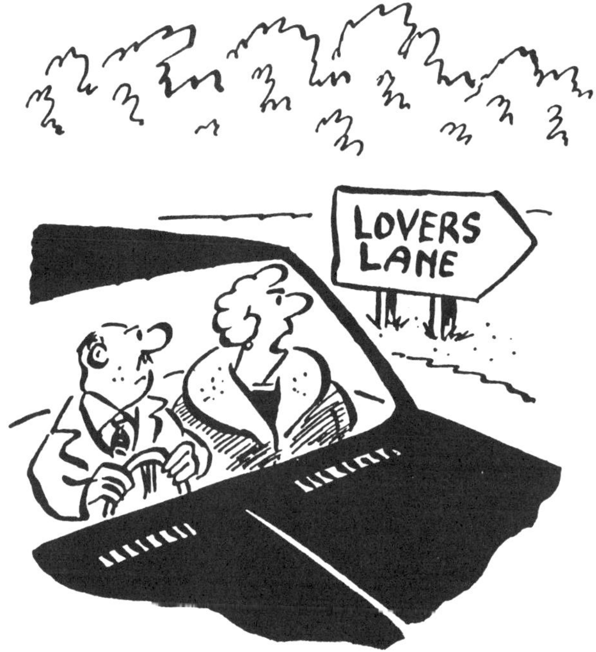

"I told you we were lost!"

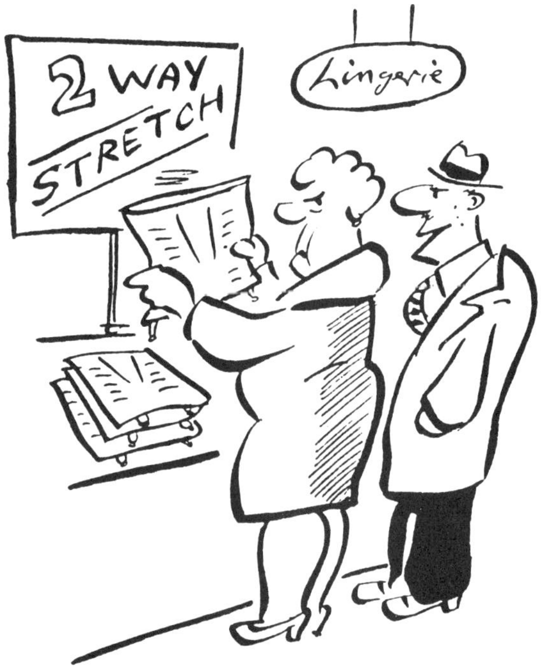

"Are you sure two ways are enough?"

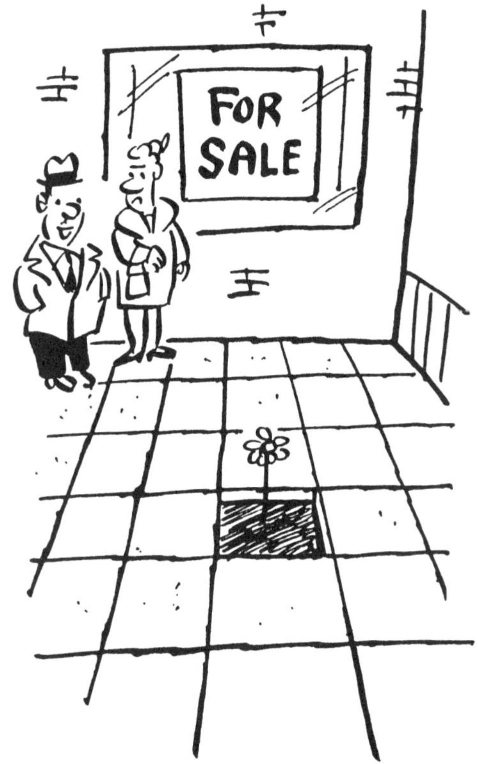

"I like the garden."

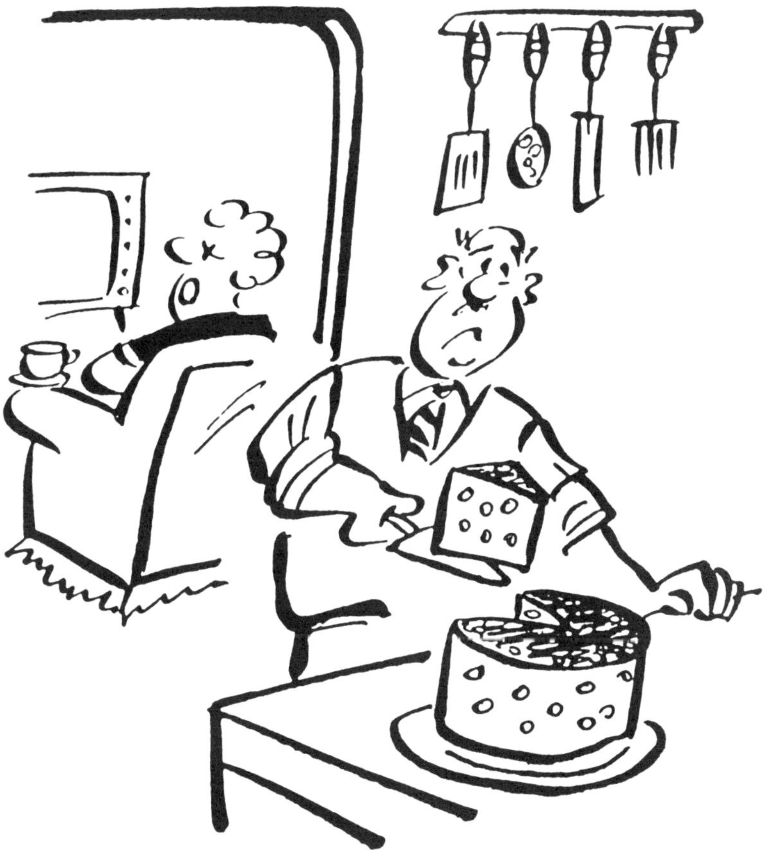

"I'm tired out. I've spent all day baking a perfect cake for the baking contest."

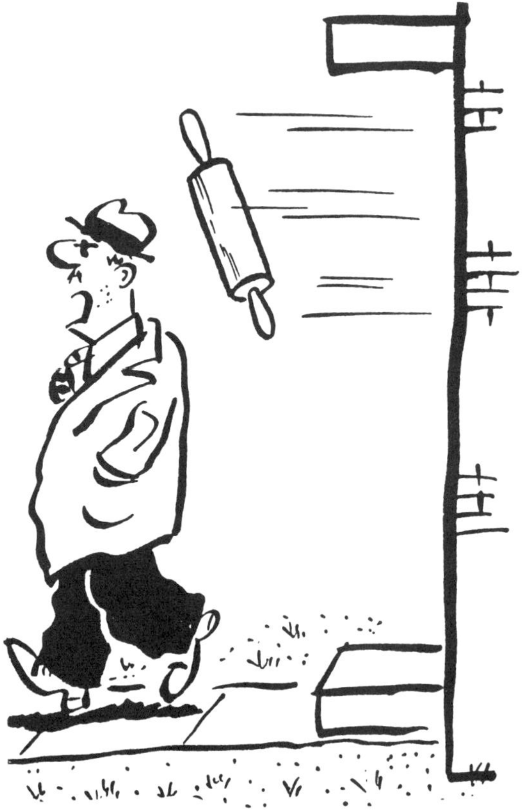

"Frankly, Scarlett, I don't give a damn."

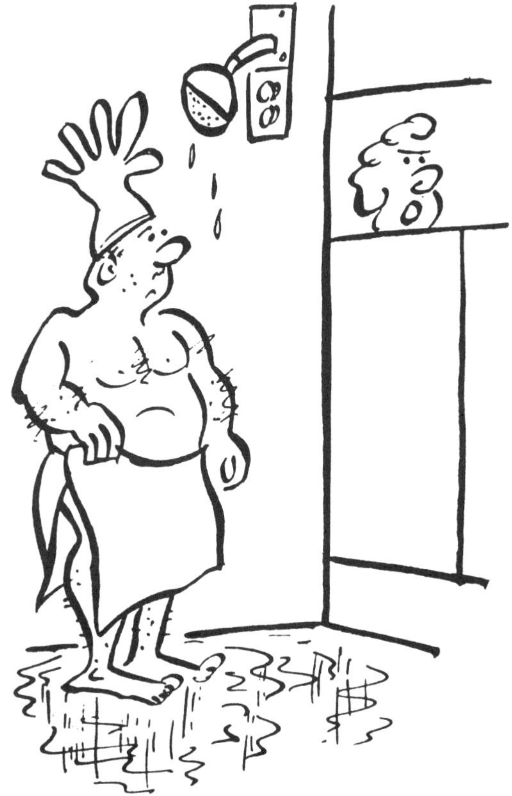

"Have you seen a rubber glove?"

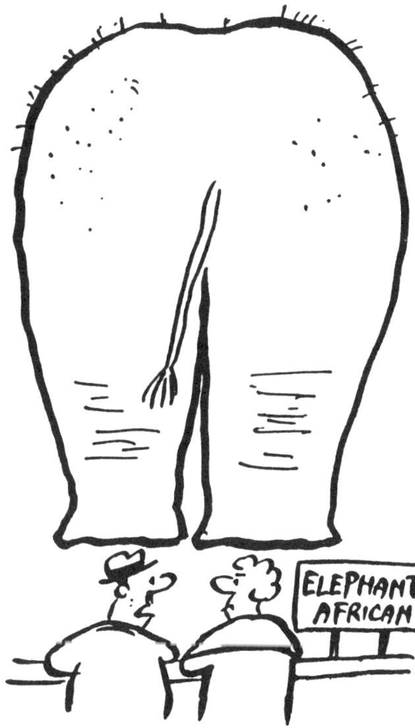

"By the way - how's your mother?"

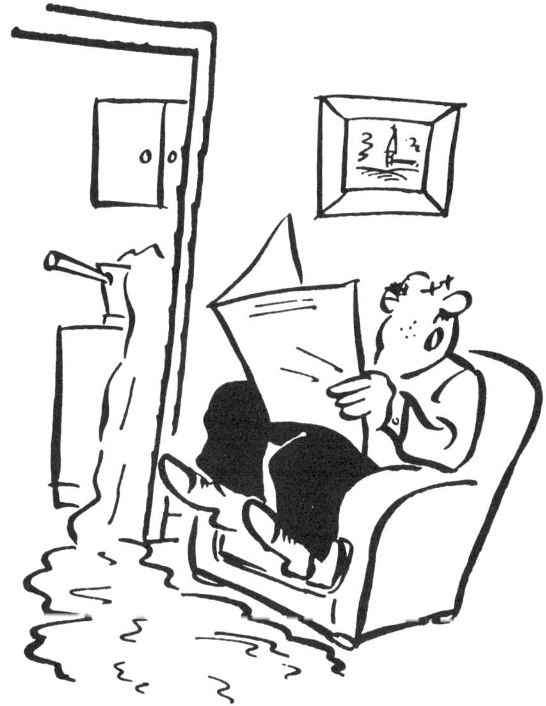

"Doris, the milk's boiling over!"

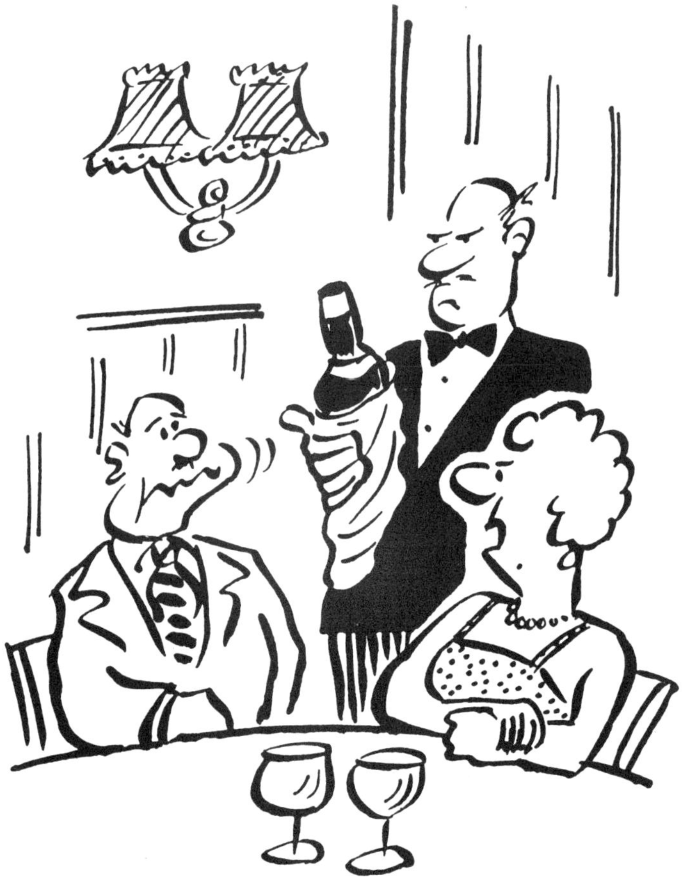

"You're supposed to just smell the cork."

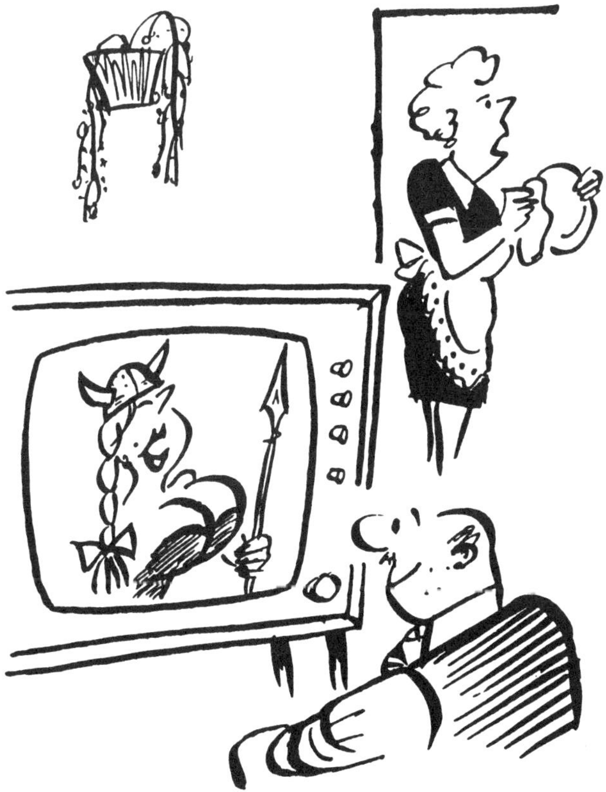

"I thought you didn't like opera?"

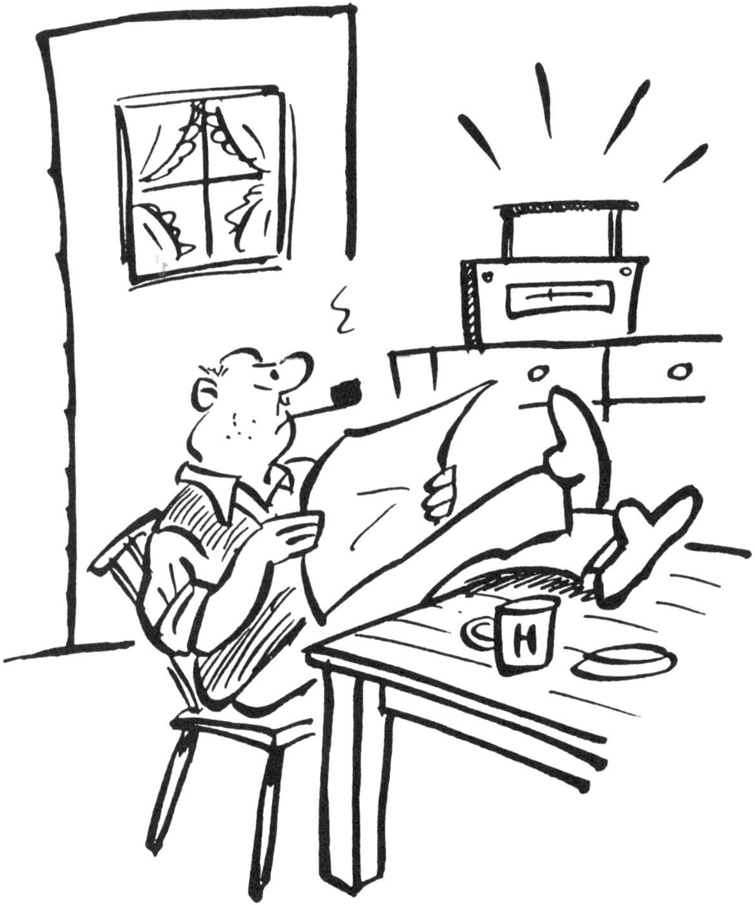

"The next request is for Horace from his wife Doris. She says please play 'Lazybones'."

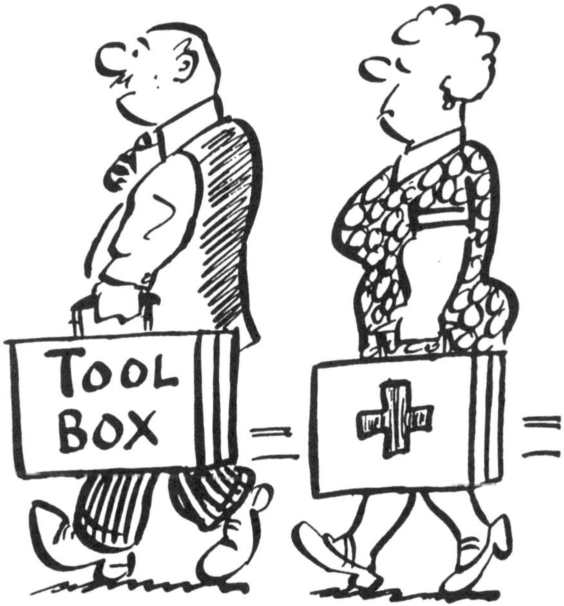

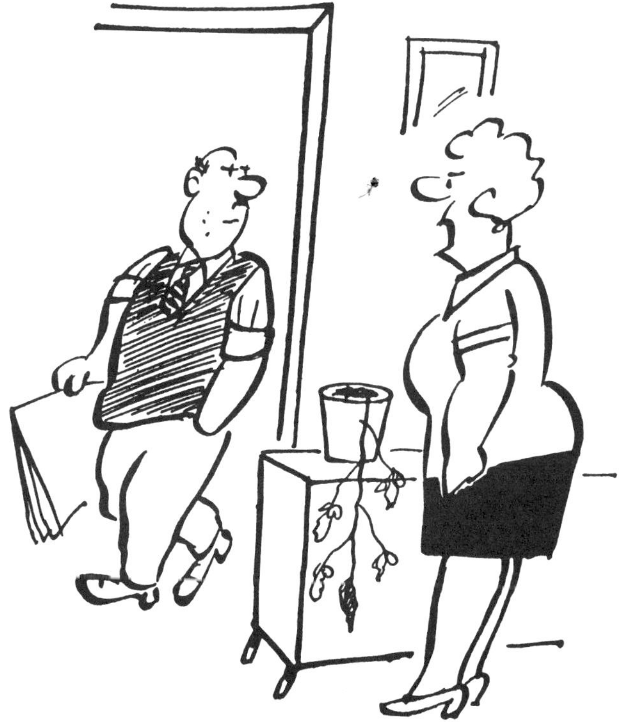

"My prize delphinium! What did you say to it?"

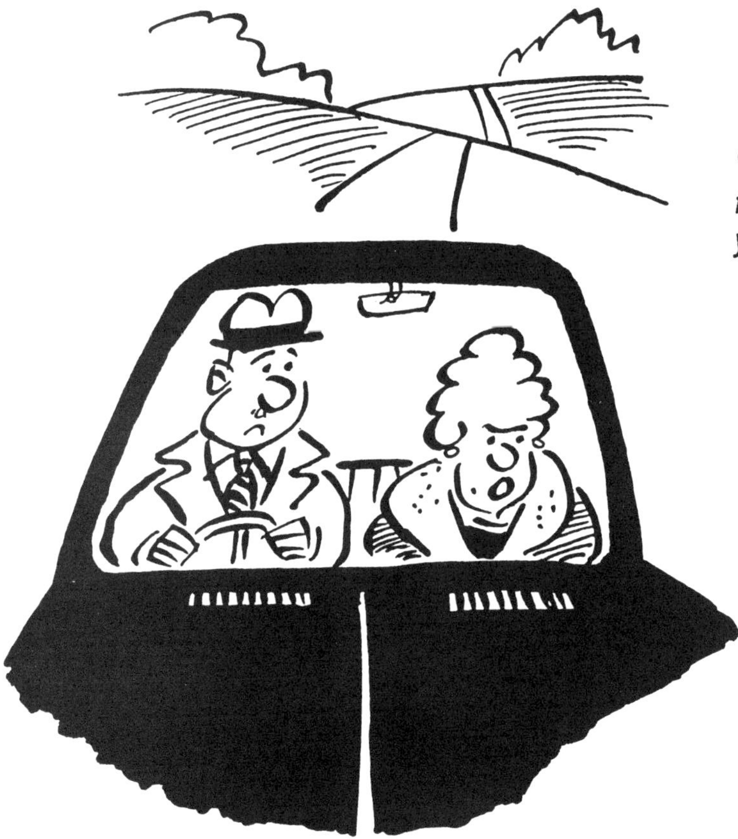

"There's no map in here but I've found twenty-five Christmas cards you didn't post last year."

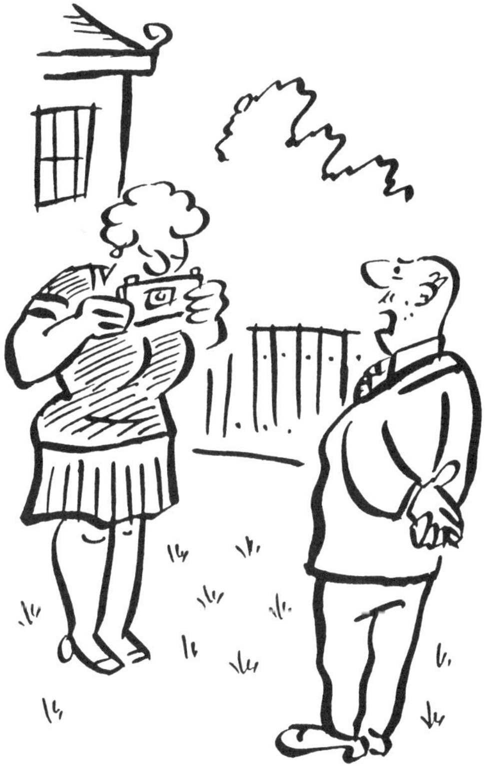

"Don't forget to tell me when to smile."

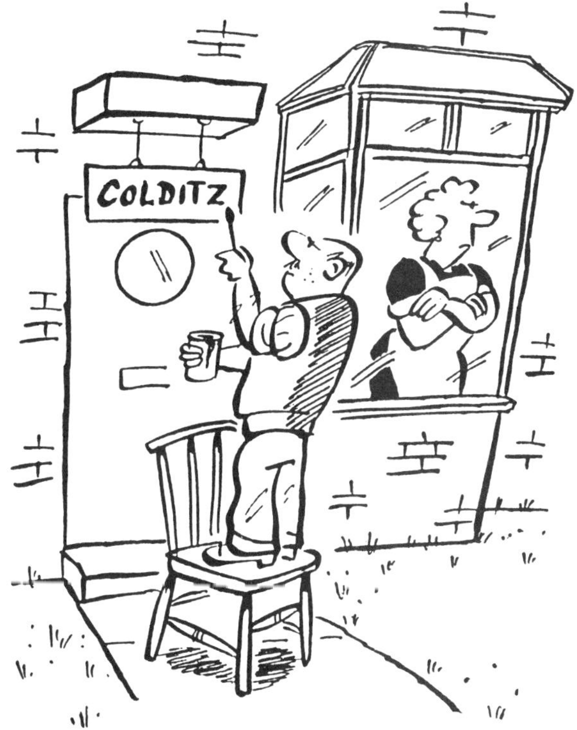

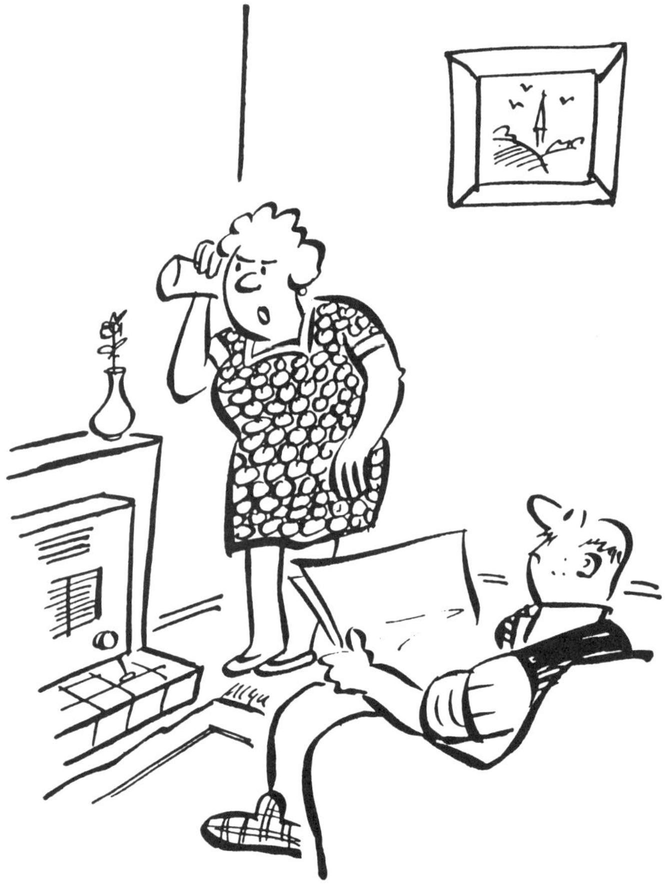

"Damn cheek, she's just called me a nosey-parker!"

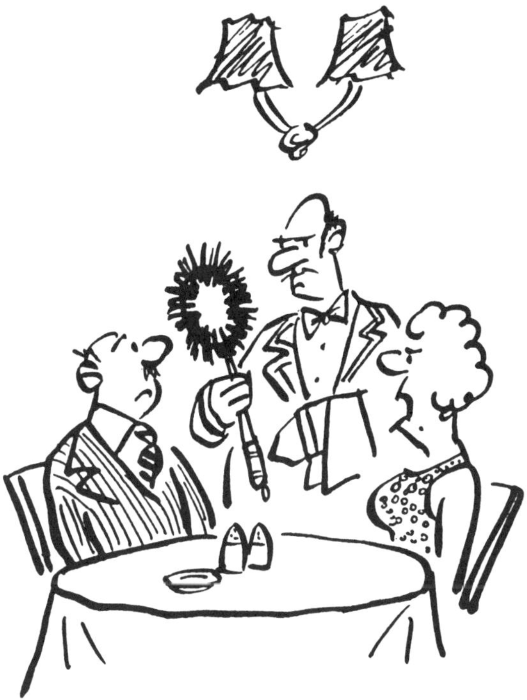

"I wish you wouldn't try and order in French!"

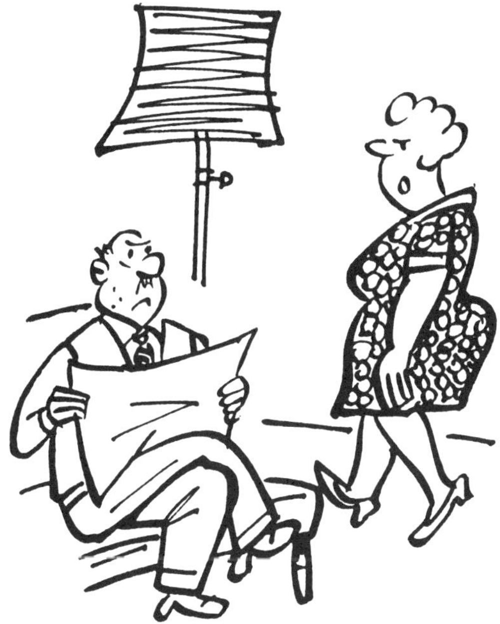

"The lawn is as high as an elephant's eye."

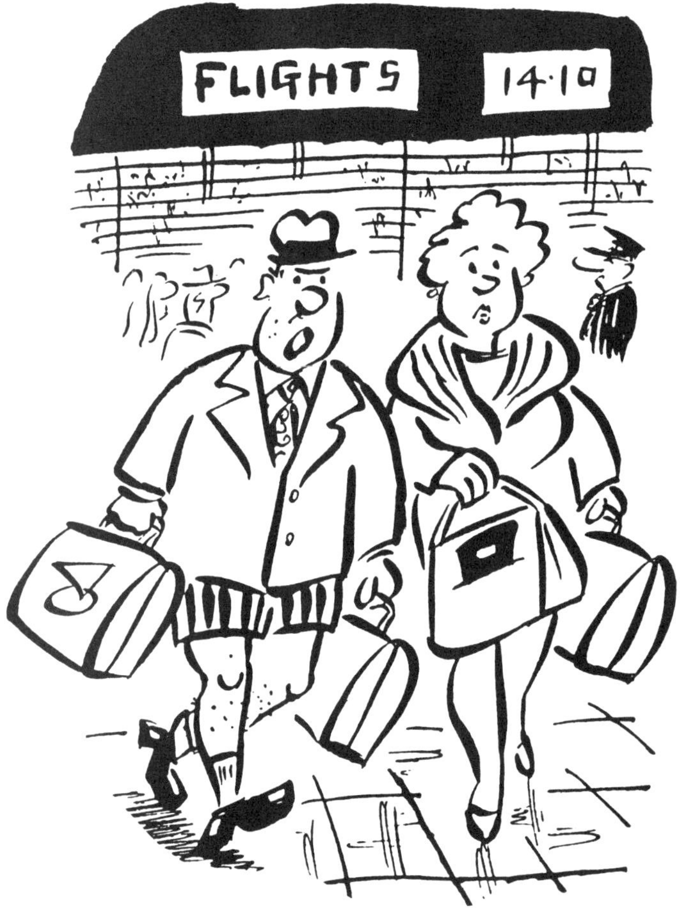

"Stop worrying! I've got the tickets in my trouser pocket."

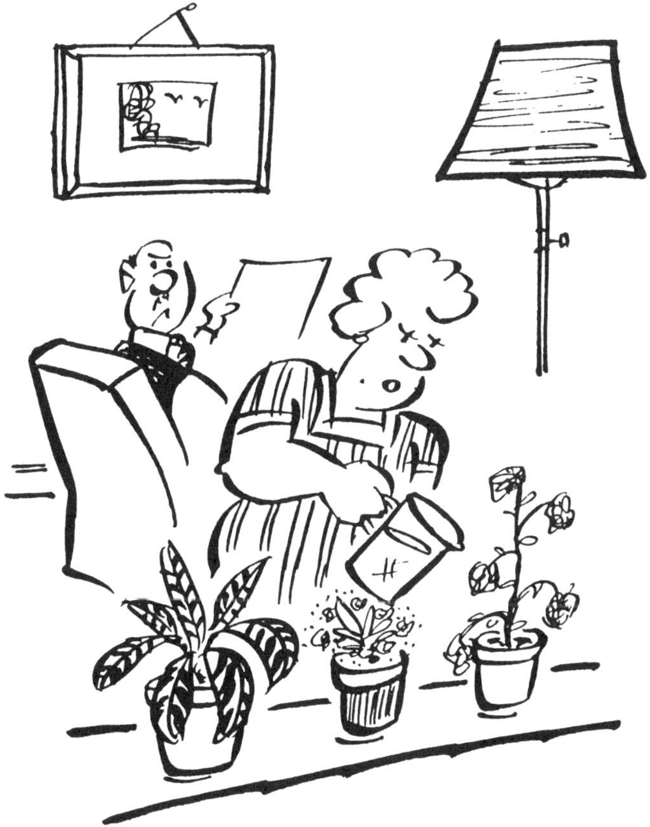

"I wish you'd talk to these plants, Horace. It would be such good fetiliser."

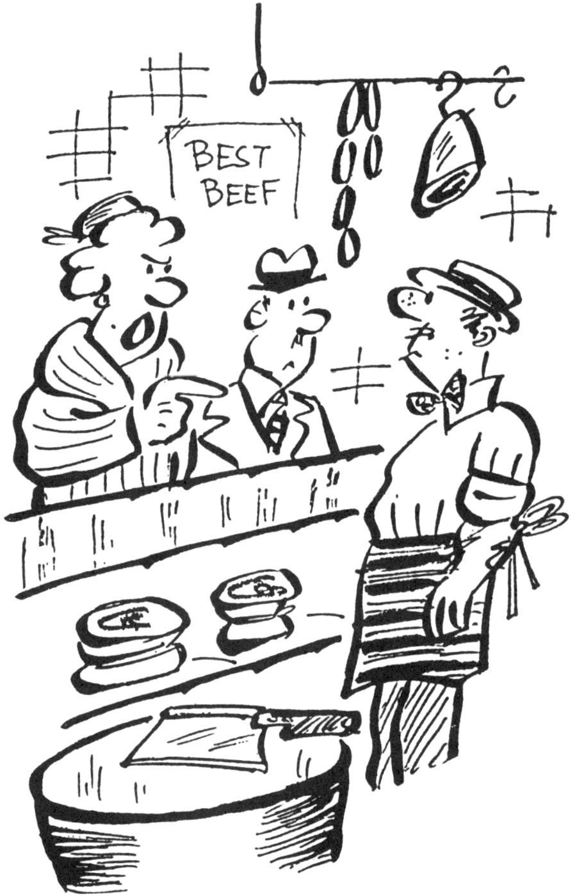

"This is my husband. If he comes in for anything just remember you are really dealing with me!"

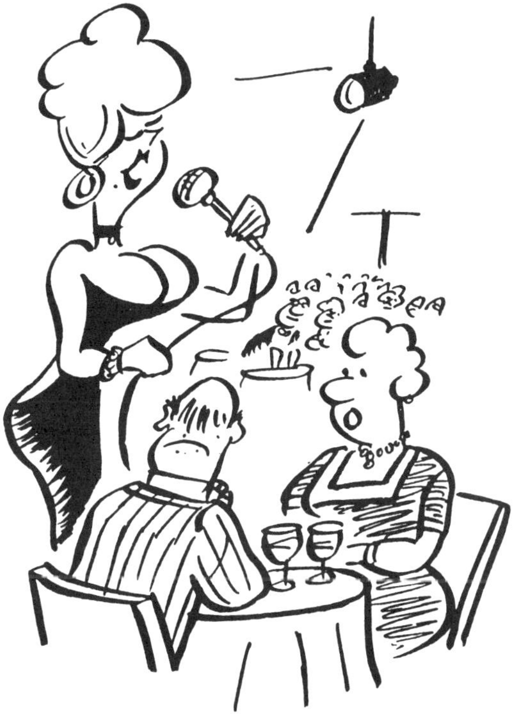

"I can sing better than her!"

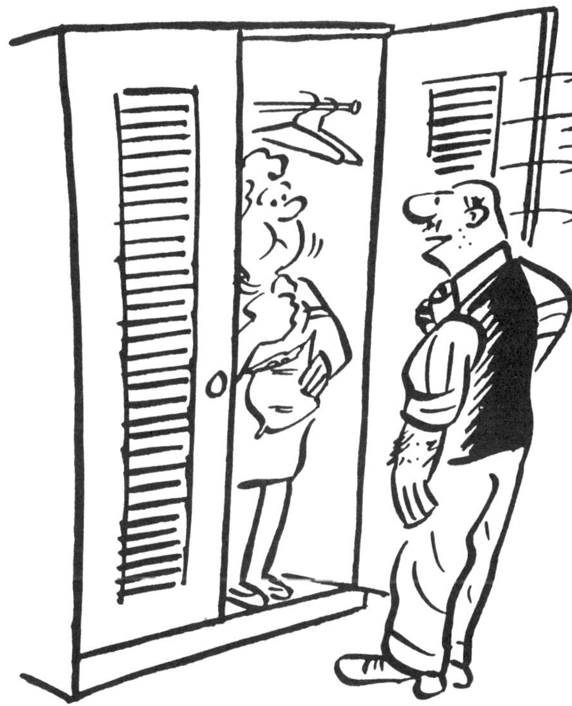

"So - you're off your diet!"

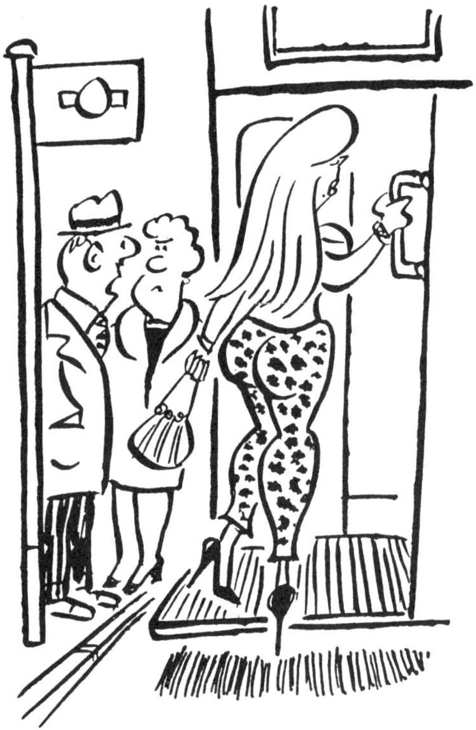

"Did I notice the number of what bus?"

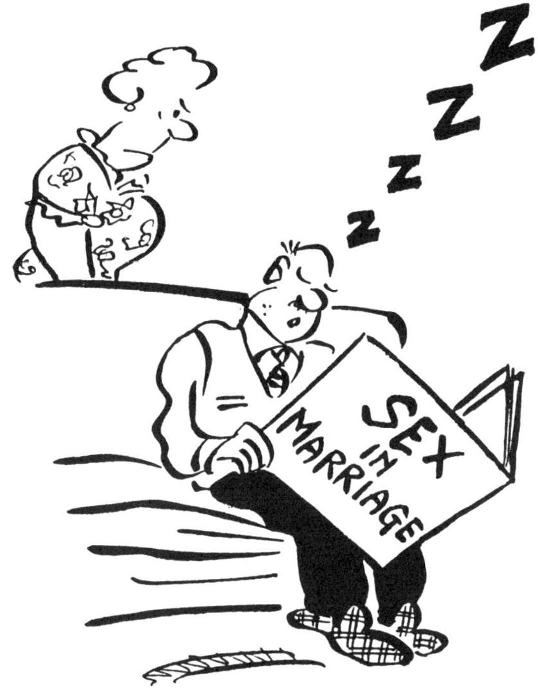

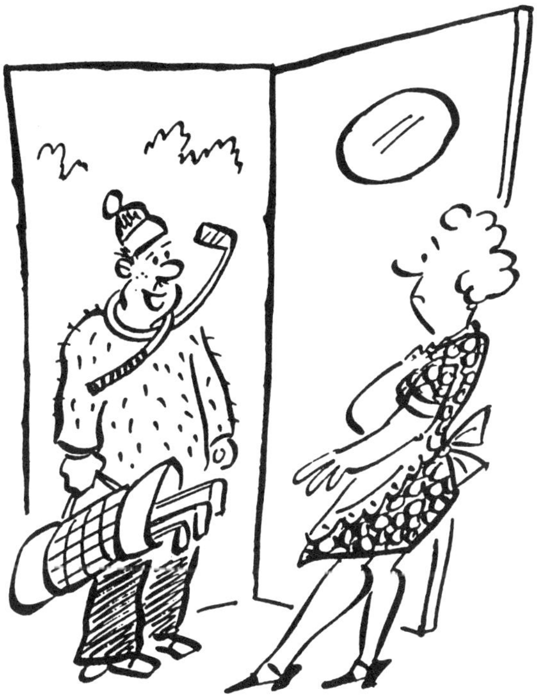

"I beat Charlie Evans!"

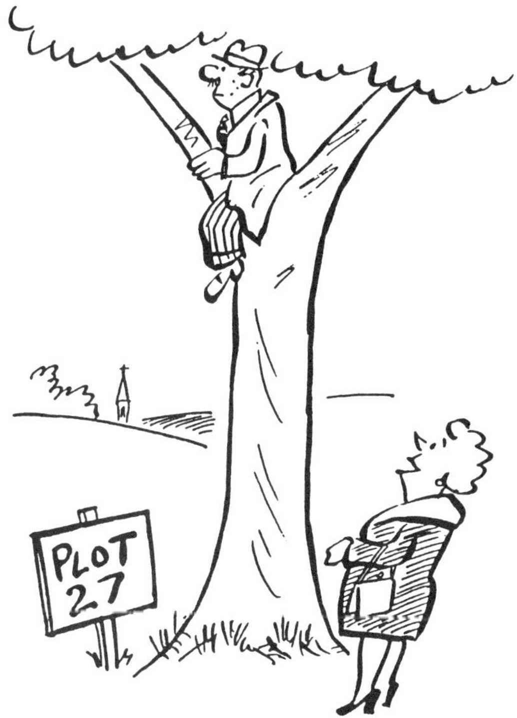

"What's the view like from the bedroom?"

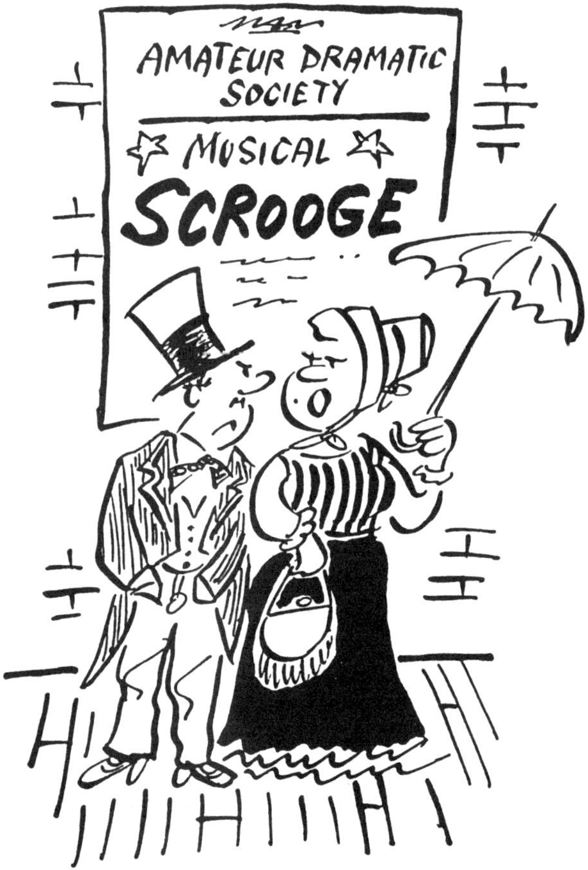

"I'm surprised they didn't ask you to play the lead."

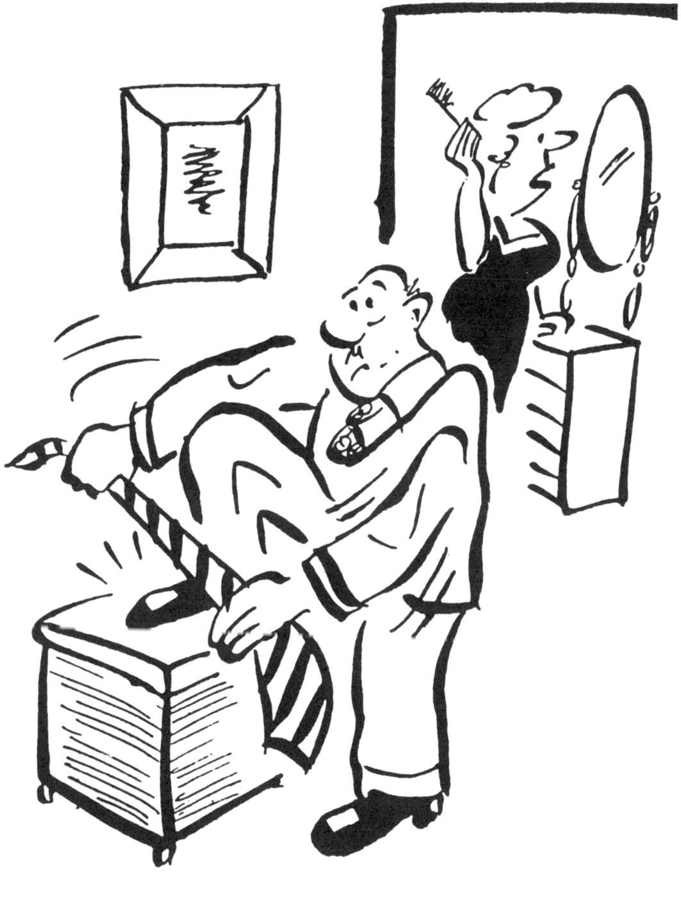

"Why don't you wear that nice striped tie mother gave you for Christmas?"

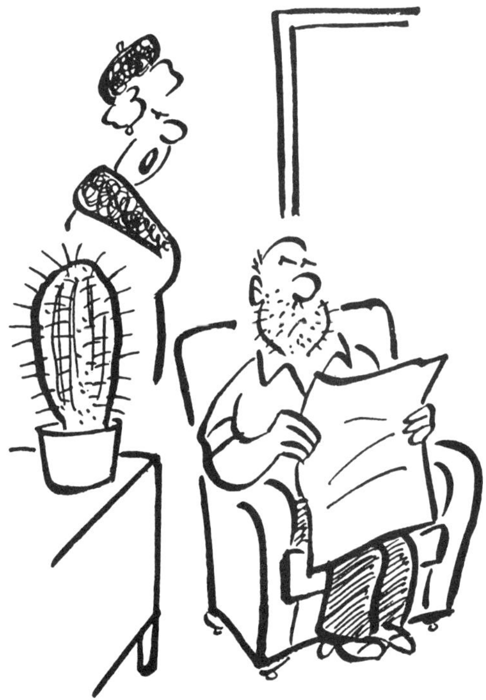

"Who's your friend?"

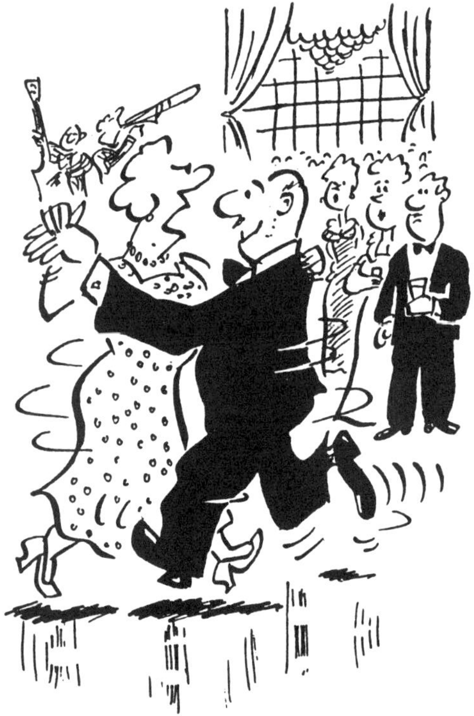

"He had a nap this afternoon."

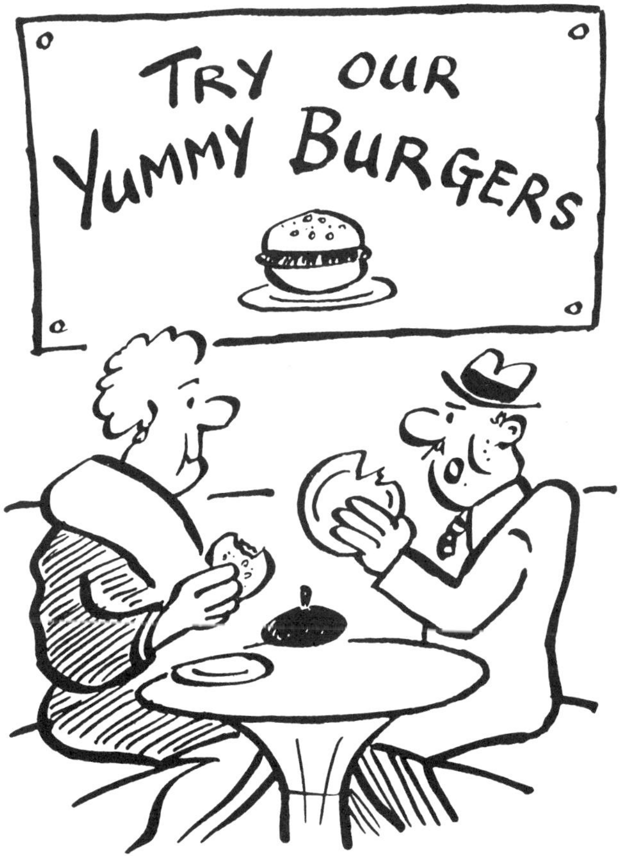

"Try the cardboard plate, it tastes better."

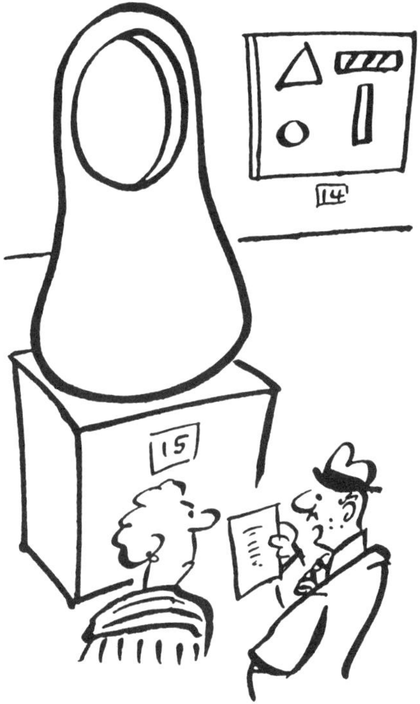

"It's called 'Woman'."

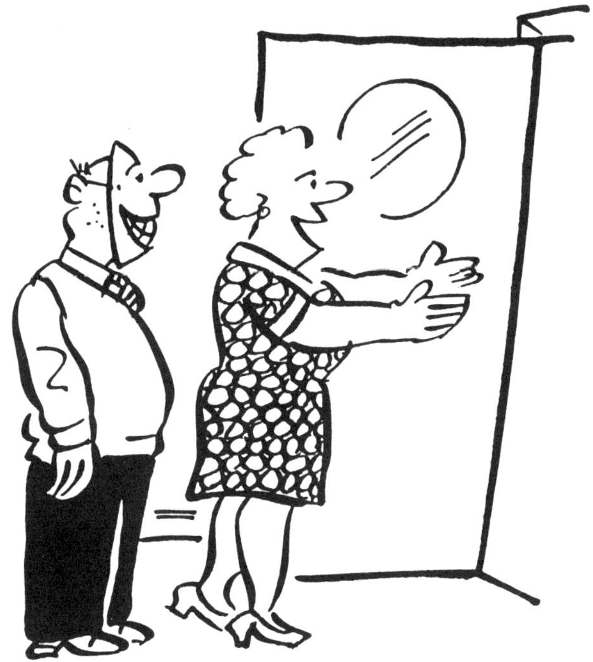

"Hello, mother!"

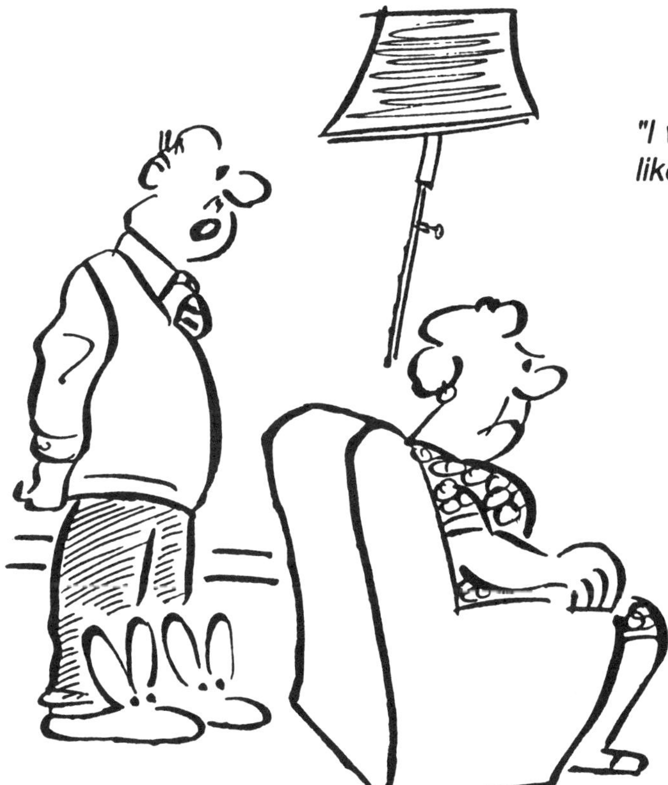

"I was only joking, Doris. I really do like them."

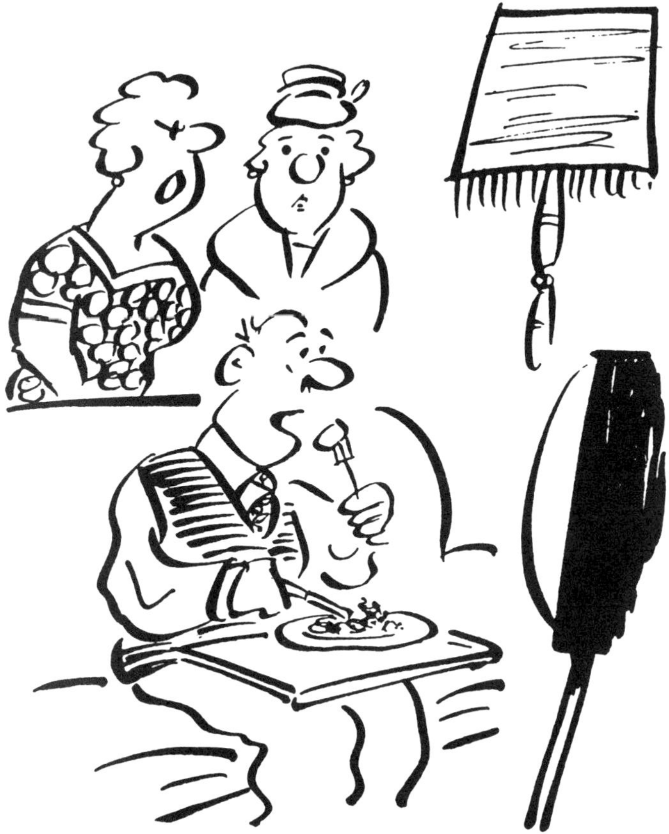

"Horace will eat anything when Dolly Parton is on."

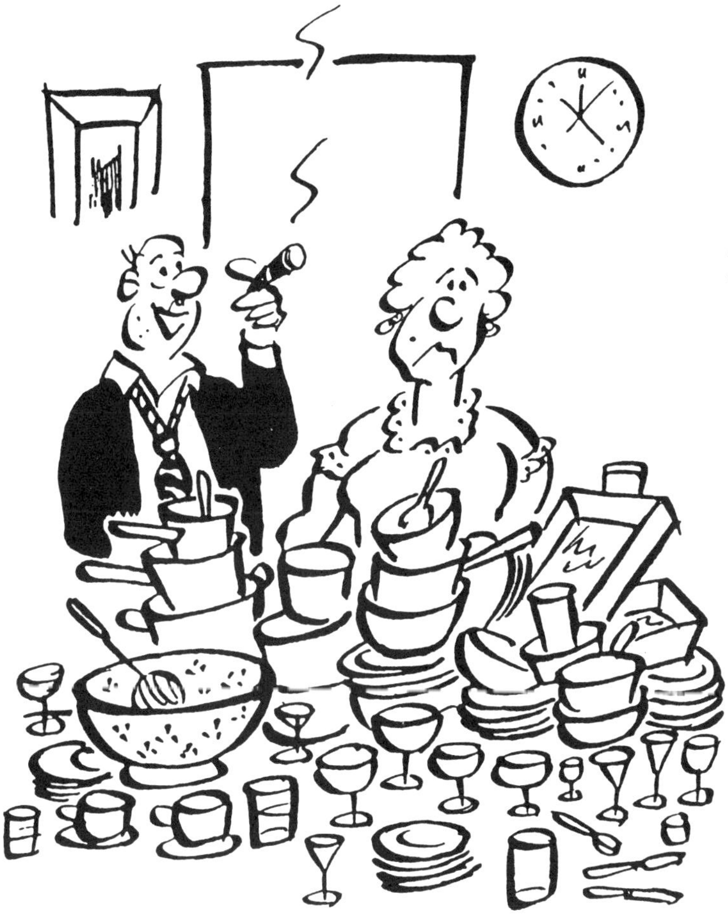

"That dinner party was so much fun I've invited them all back again next week."

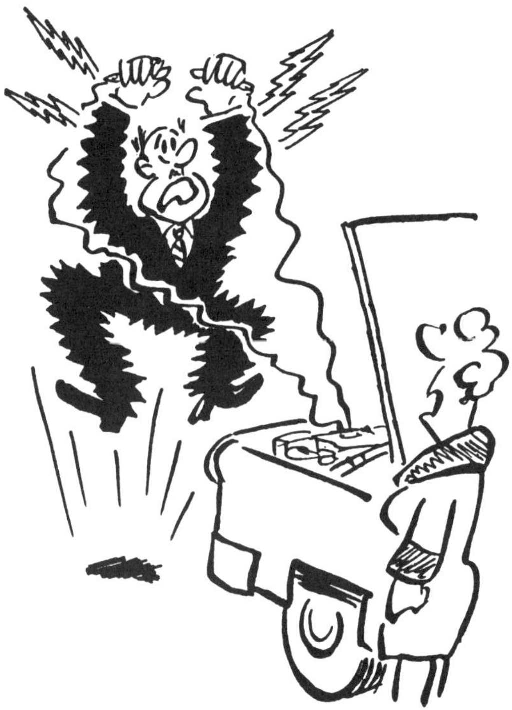

"So that's why they call them jump-leads!"

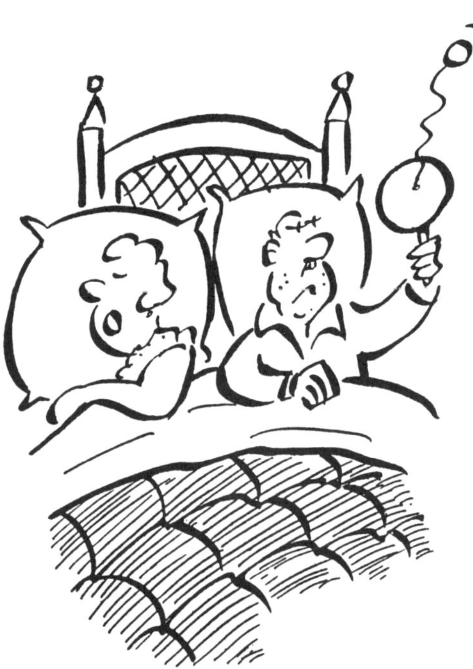

"I told you not to drink all that coffee."

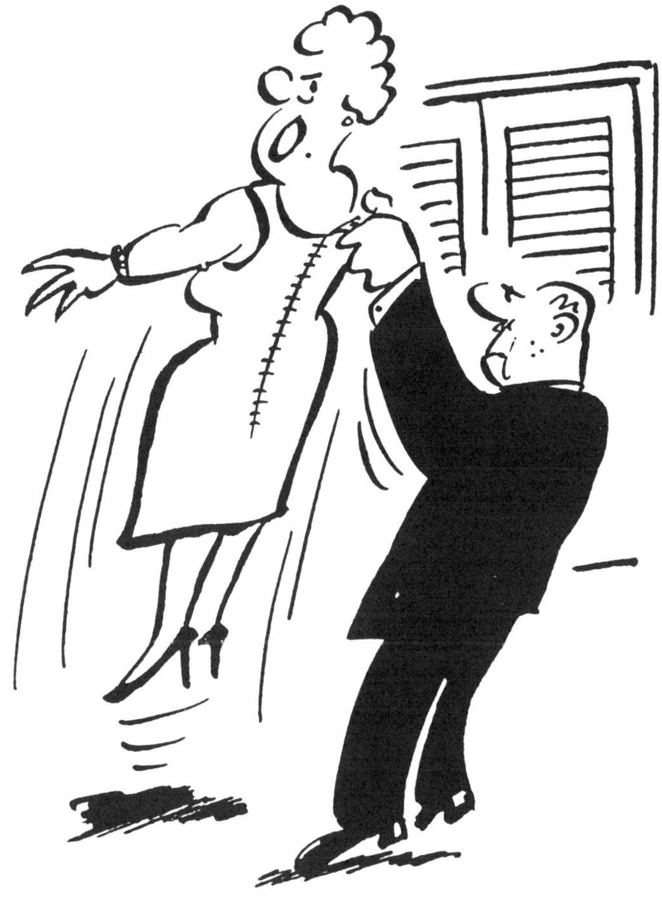

"That's not the way you used to zip my dresses up when we first got married!"

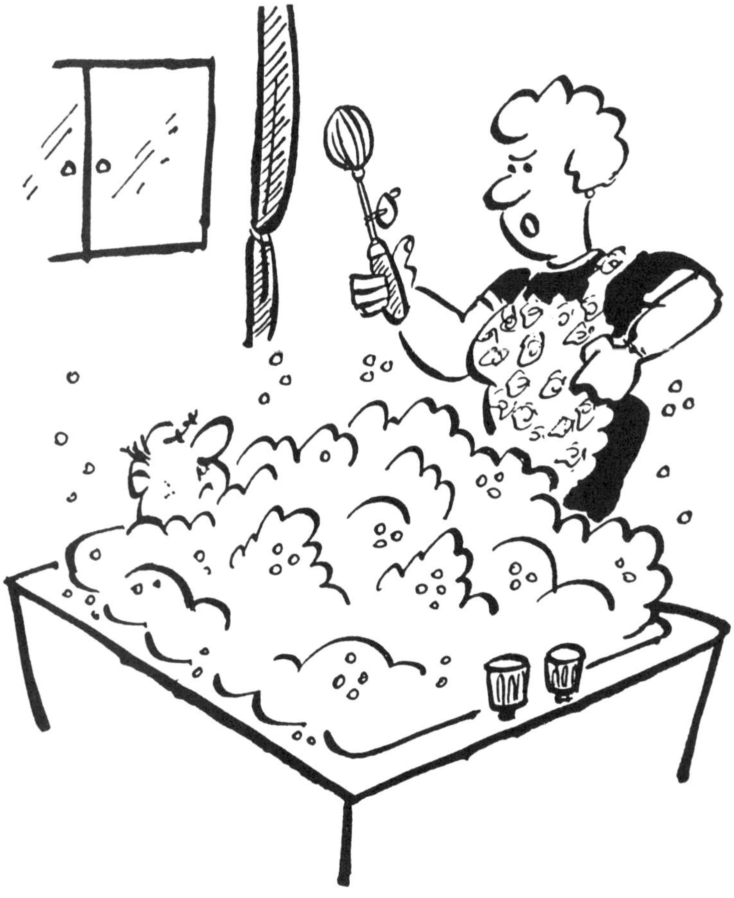

"What's my egg-whisk doing in here?"

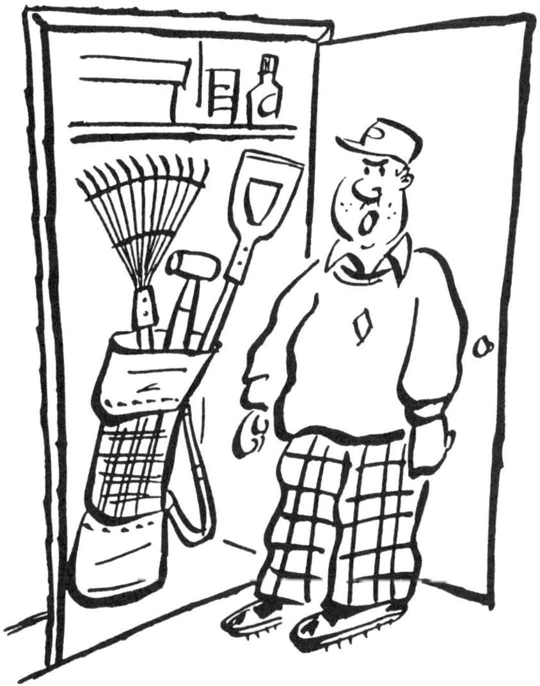

"Very funny!"

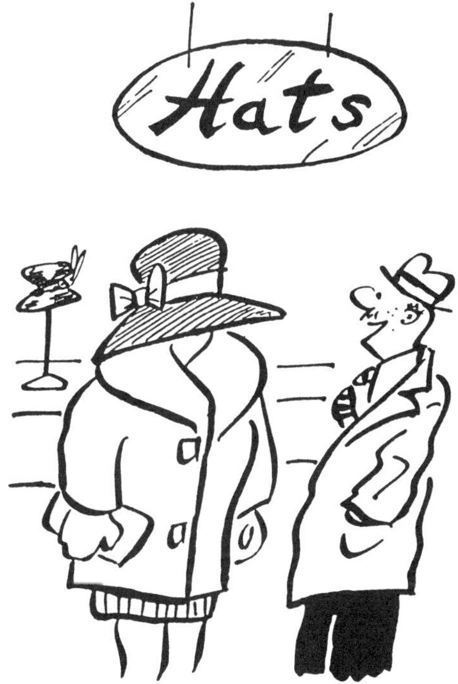

"I like it!"

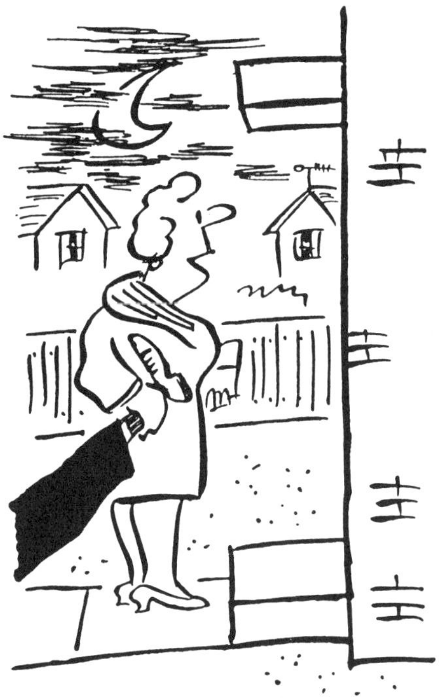

"Hello, Mother - it's me and Horace."

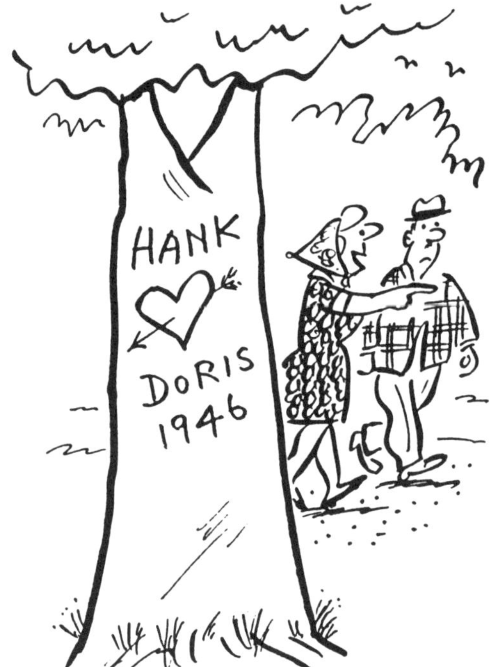

"Let's go this way, Horace."

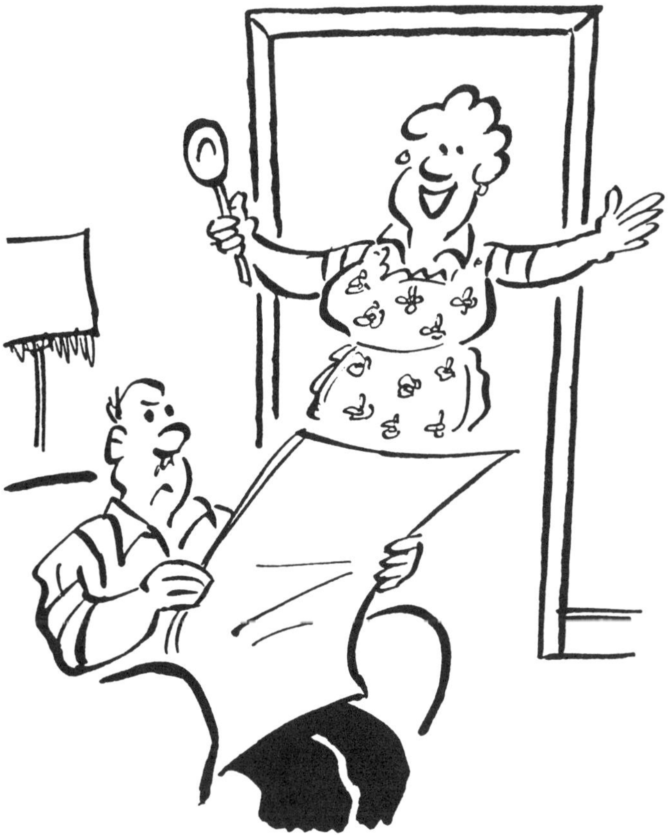

"Tonight it's 'Beef à la Doris' - in other words hash."

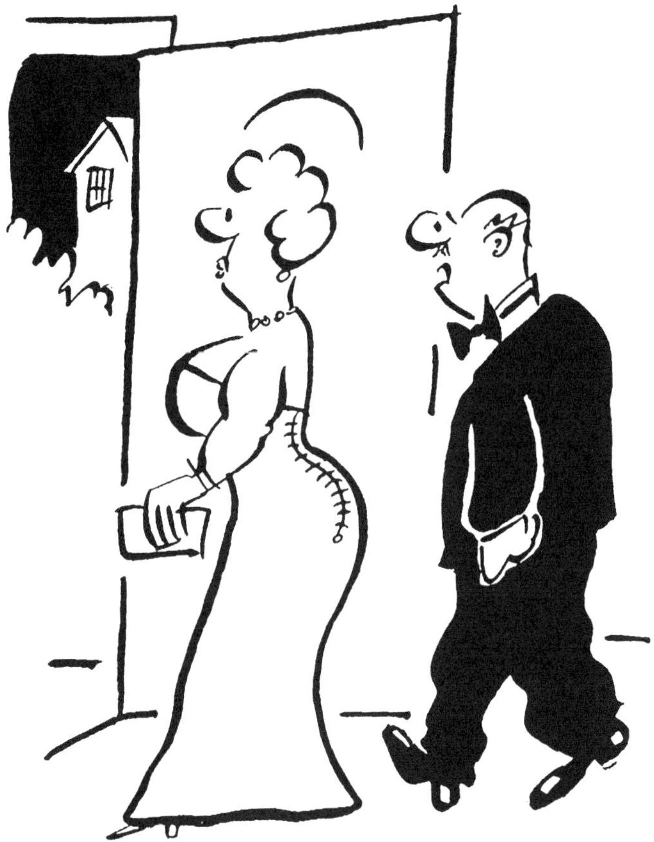

"You realise this is a sit down function, don't you?"

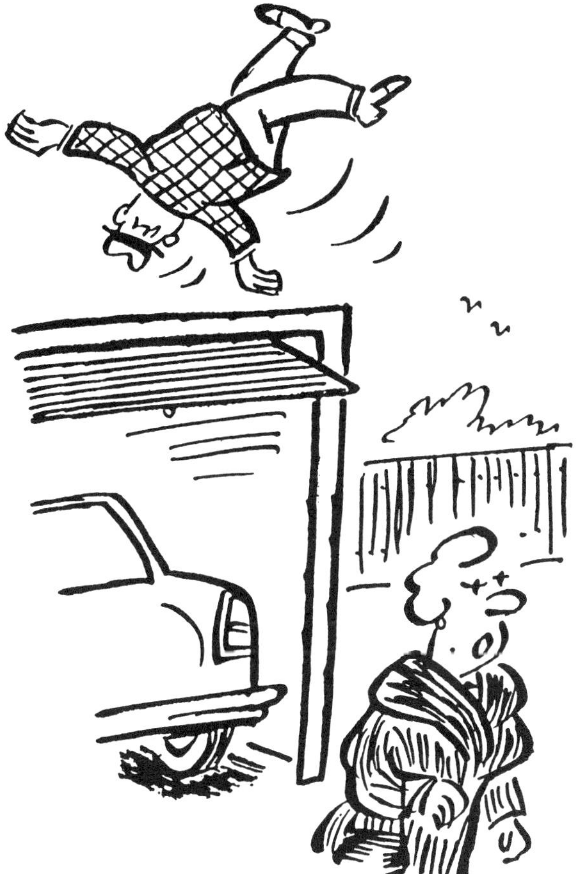

"By the way Horace, I've oiled the garage door."

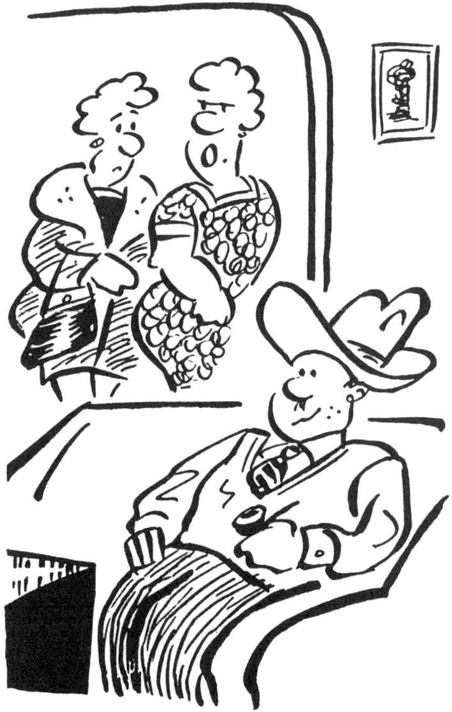

"It's a season of John Wayne films."

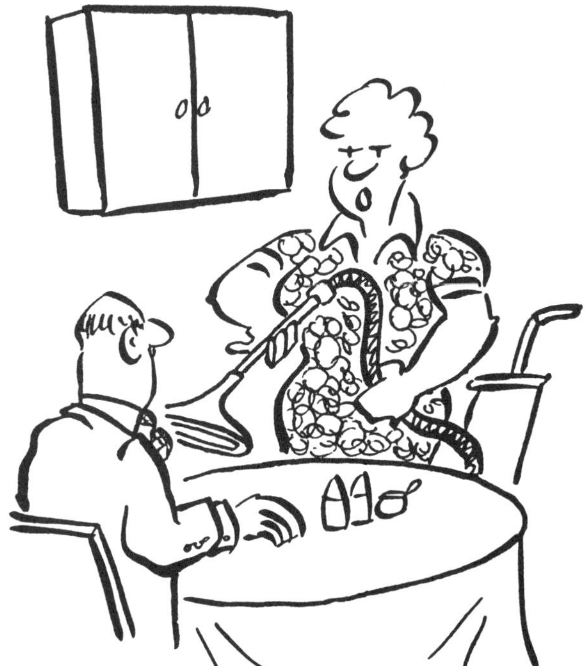

"Do you want dessert?"

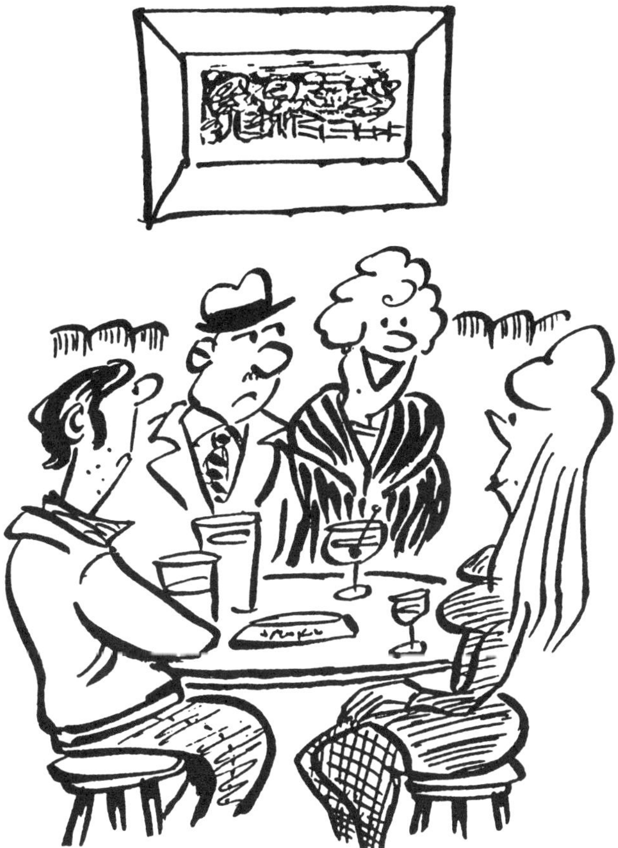

"When my husband and I were courting it was just like Romeo and Juliet - my father hated him."

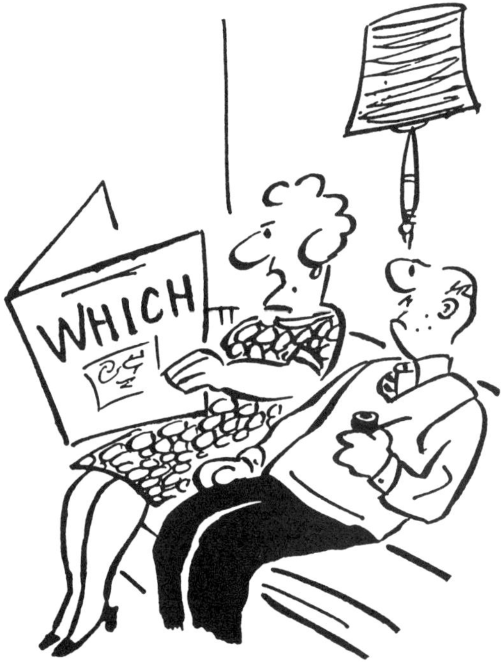

"I wish they'd done one on husbands."

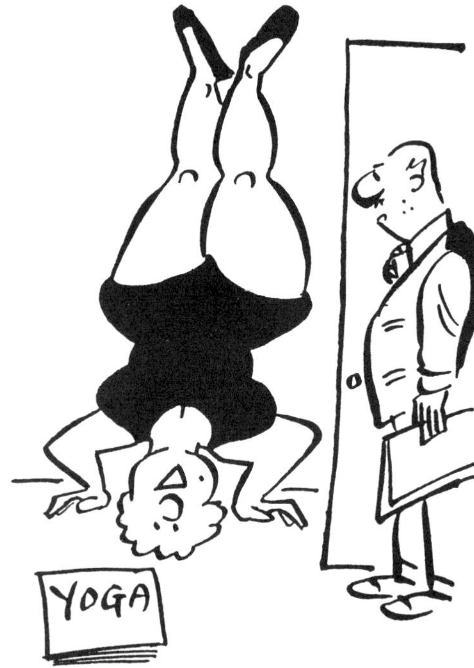

"Look, Horace - 42", 28", 36"."

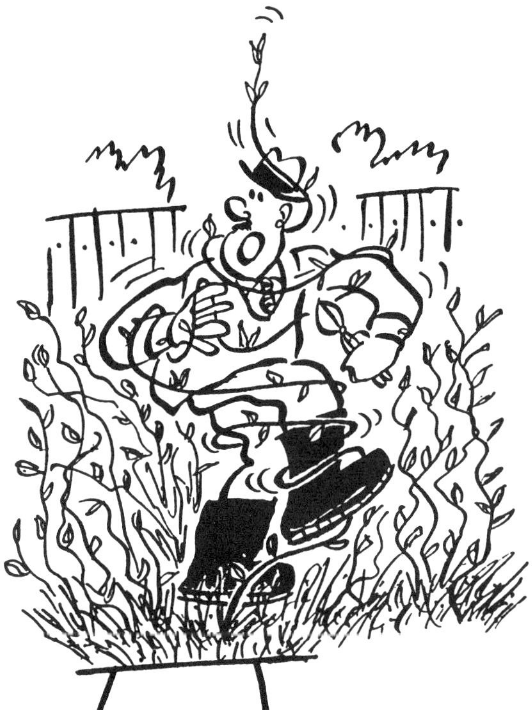

"Quick, Doris - get the weedkiller!"

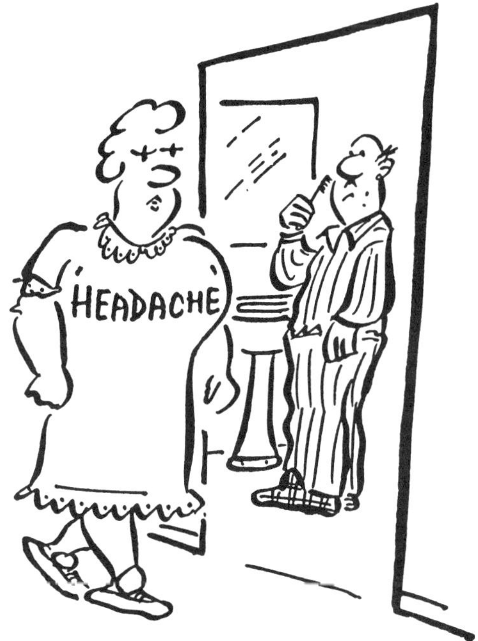

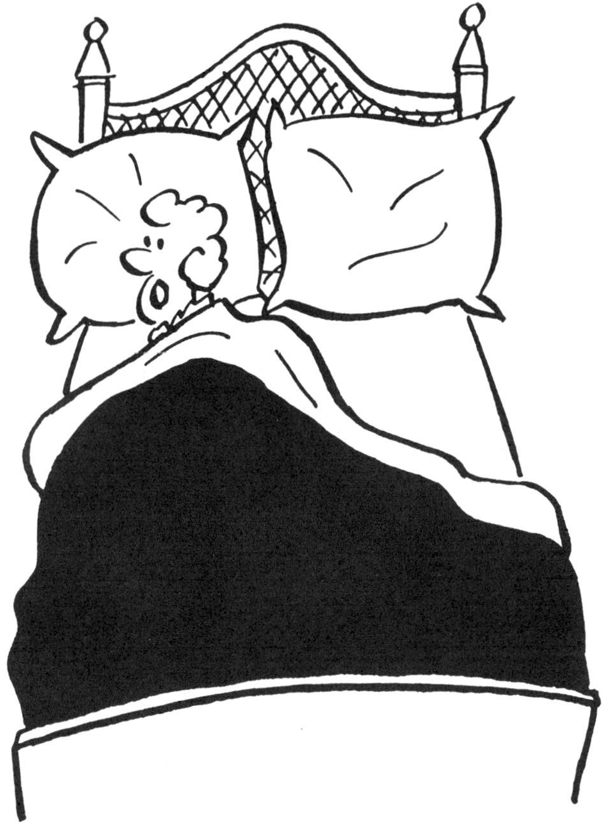

"Horace, there's somebody downstairs in the kitchen - I heard the fridge door open."

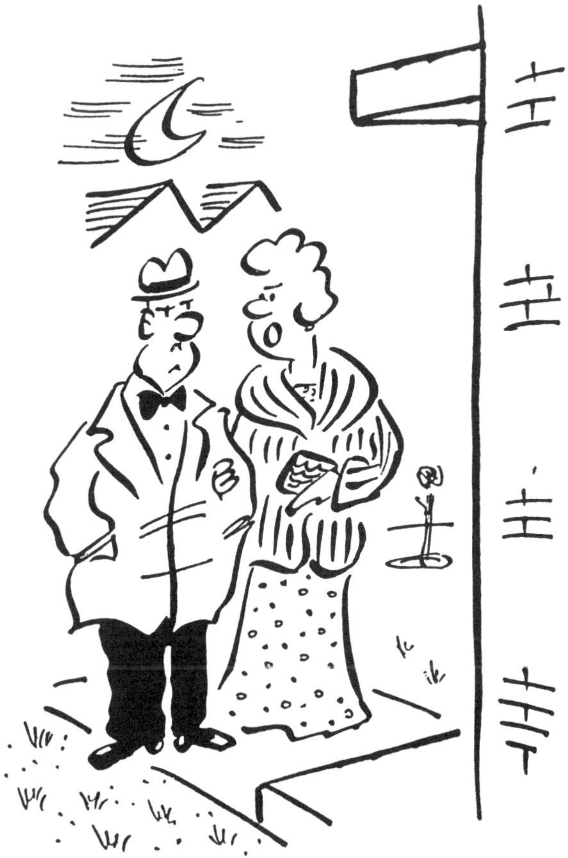

"Just remember to keep off politics, religion and haemorrhoids."

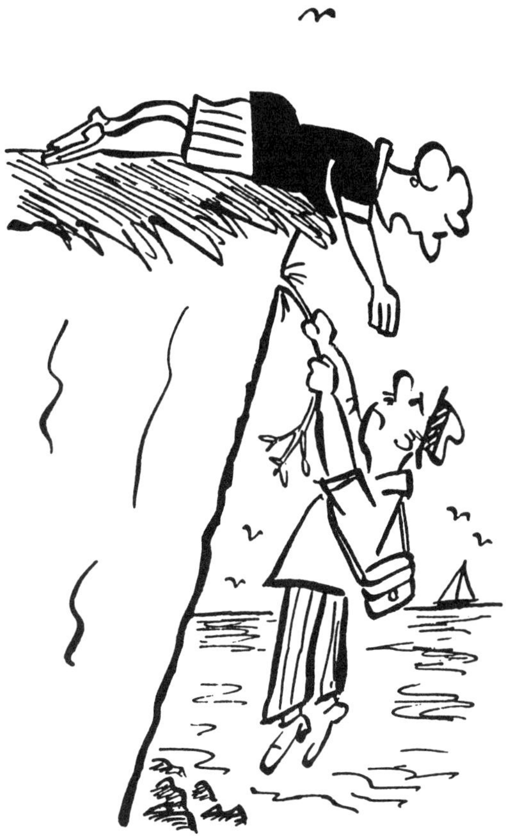

"Don't panic, pass me up the camera and return tickets."

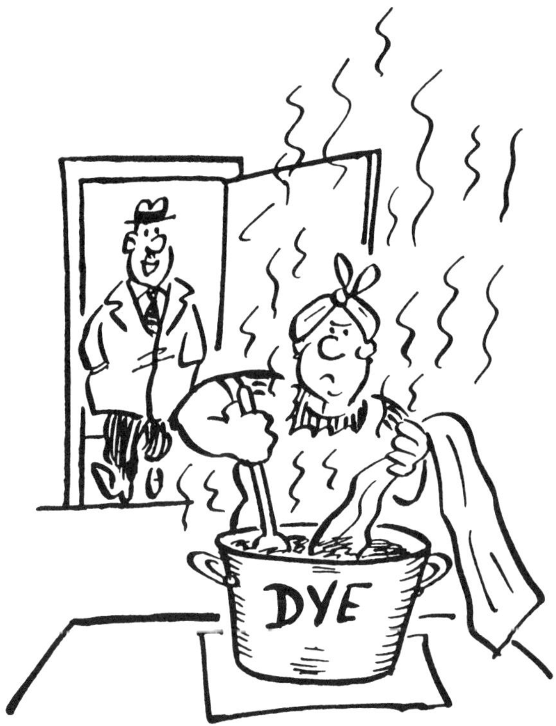

"Mmmm - that smells good."

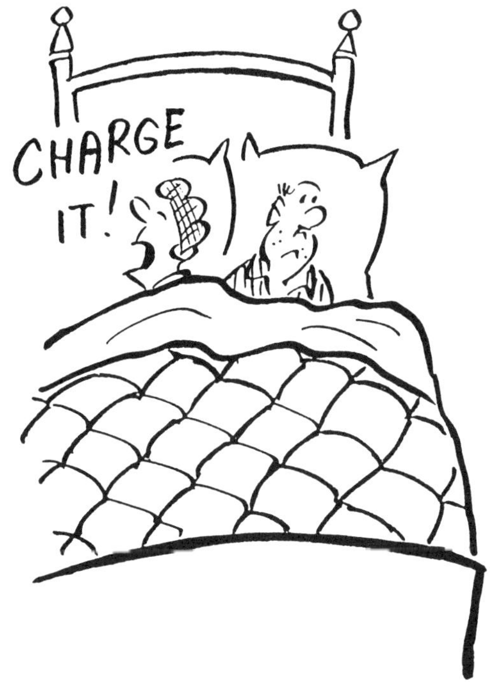

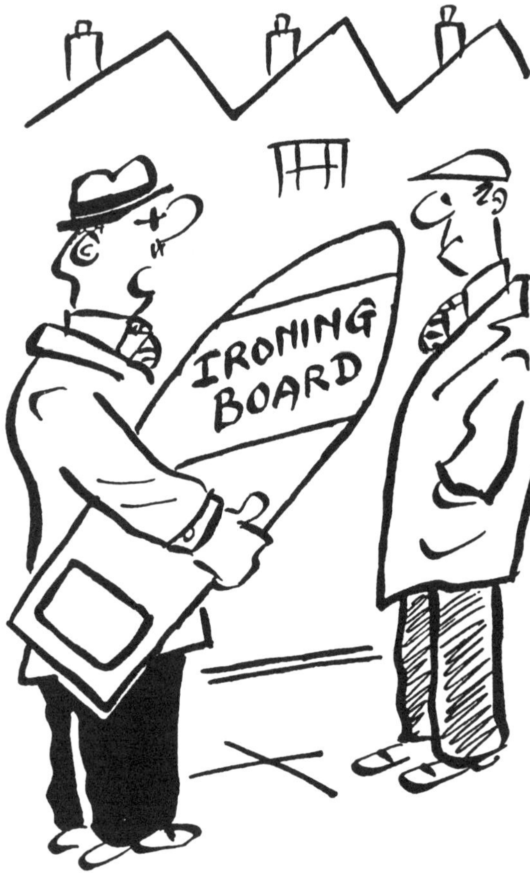

"It's a surprise present for Doris - she's expecting a diamond."

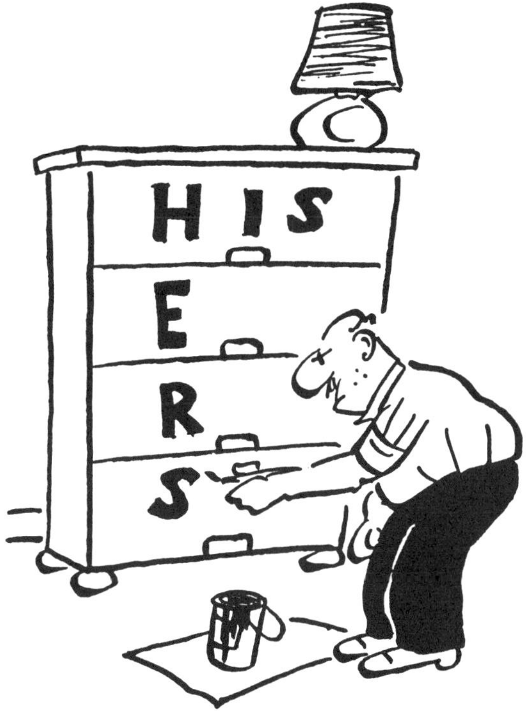

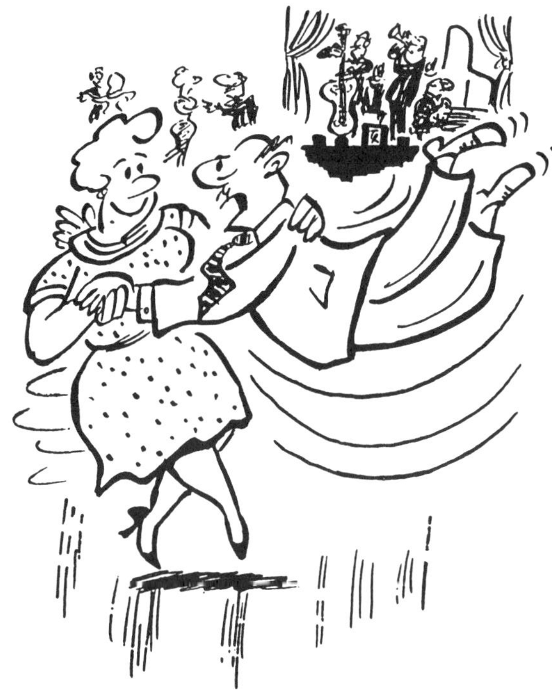

"You're leading again Doris!"

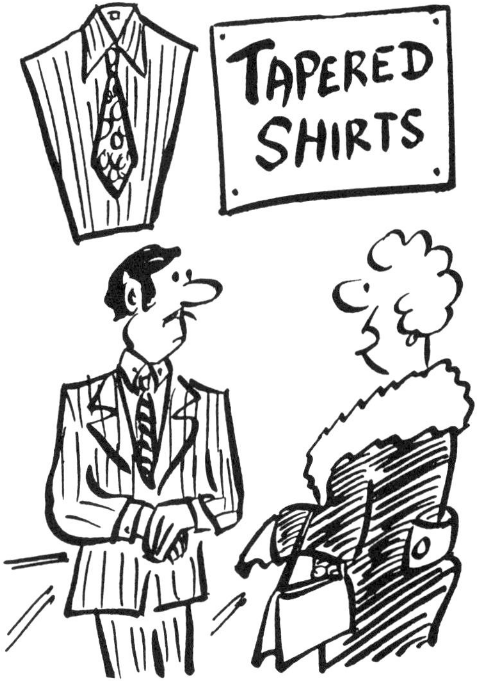

"Do you have any that taper the other way?"

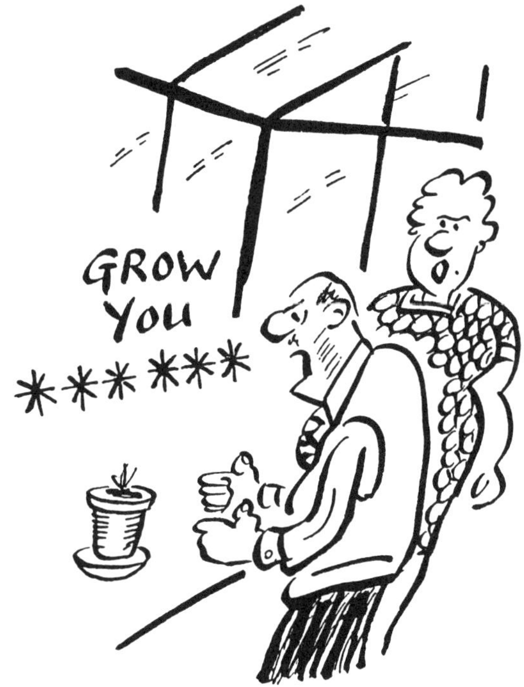

"That's not the way to talk to it!"

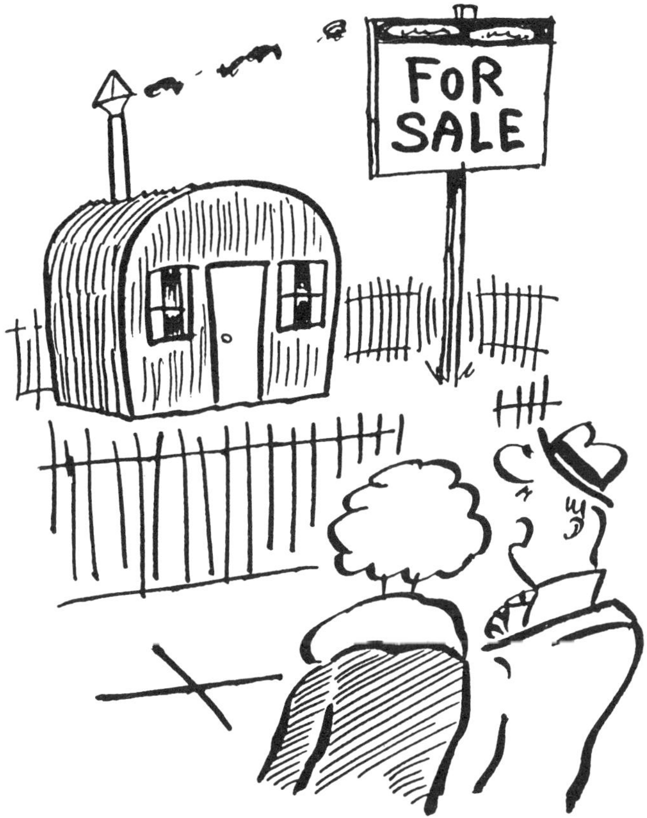

"I asked them to send us something in our price range."

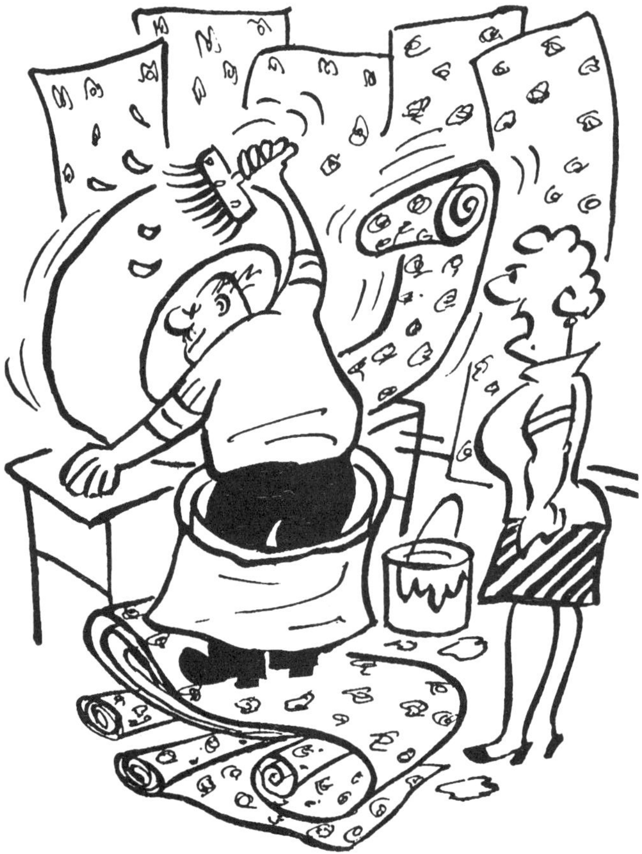

"I told you to do the wallpapering before you went to the pub!"

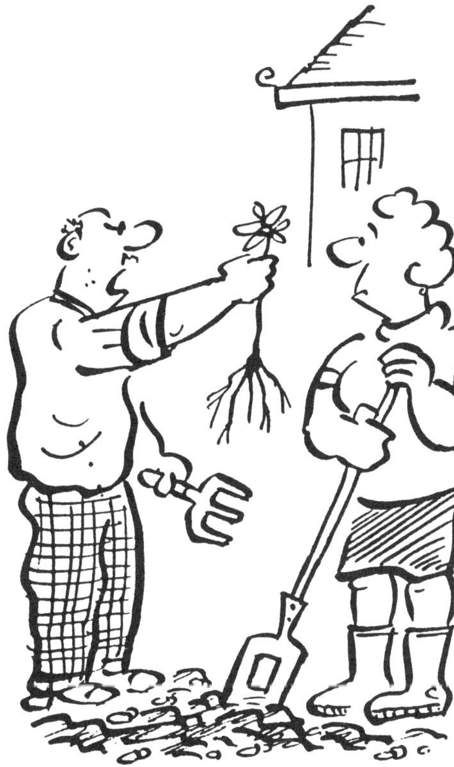

"Is this a weed?"

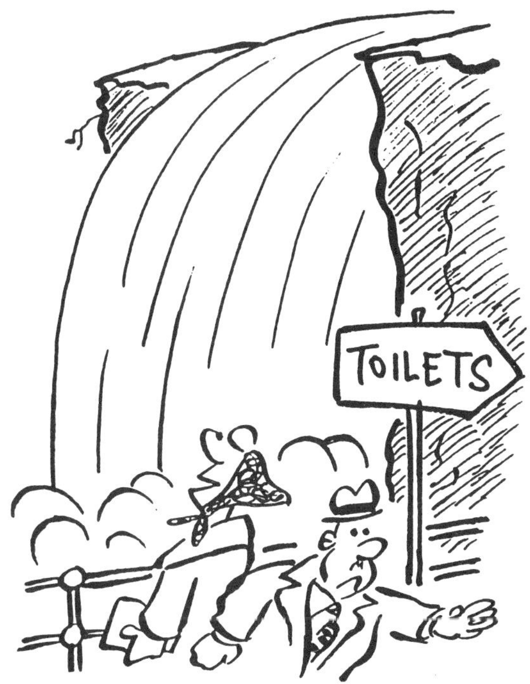

"Isn't the water-fall beautiful, Horace?"

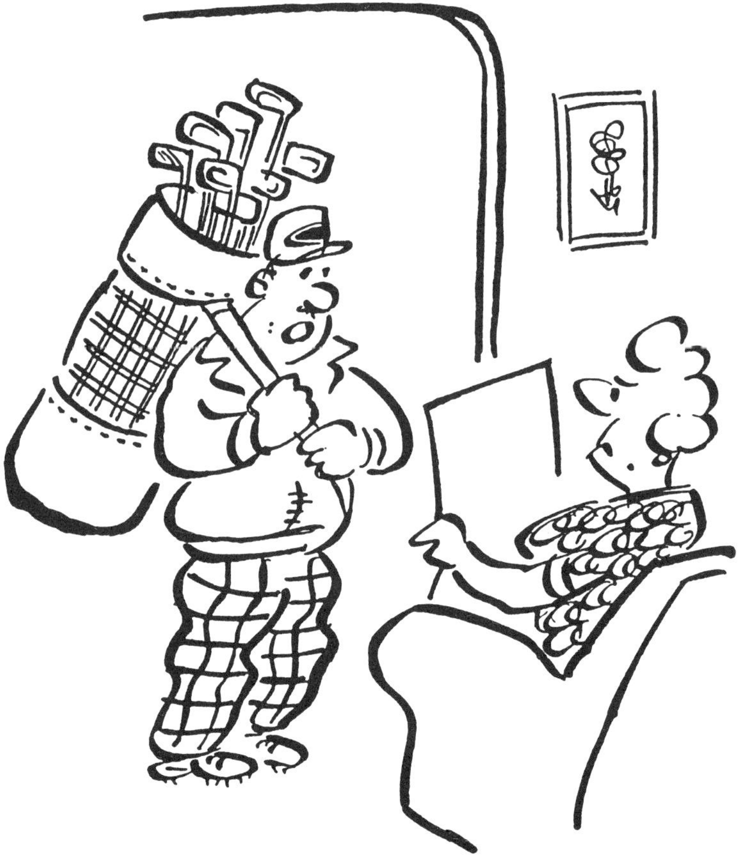

"Alright, if you don't fancy a game what about caddying for me?"

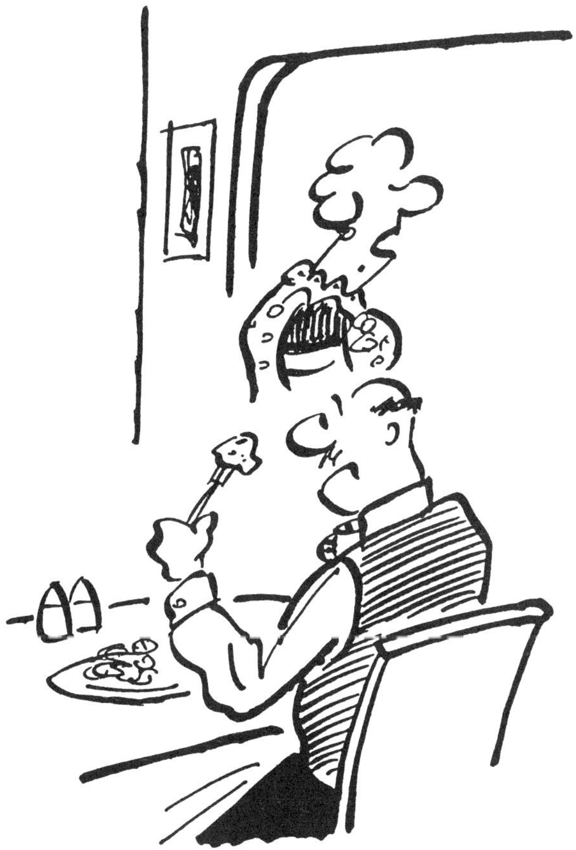

"The little grey bits are off the non-stick frying pan."

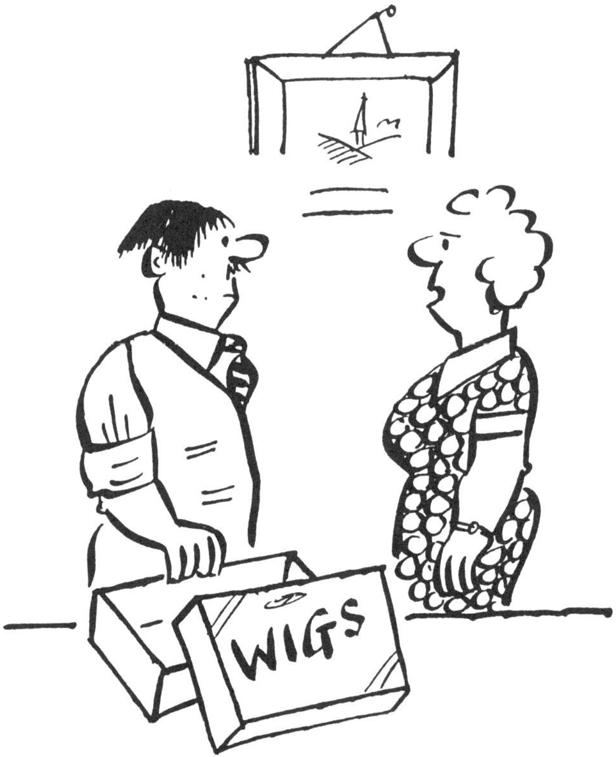

"I think it makes you look twenty years sillier!"

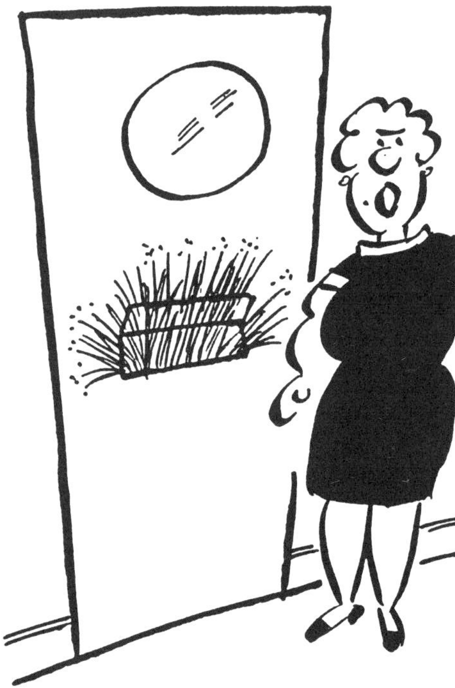

"When are you going to cut the lawn?"

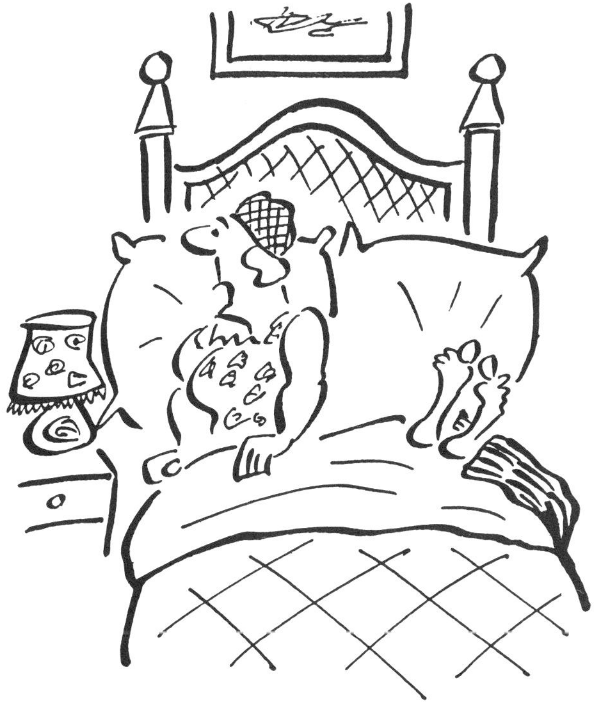

"Horace! Did you hear a bump?"

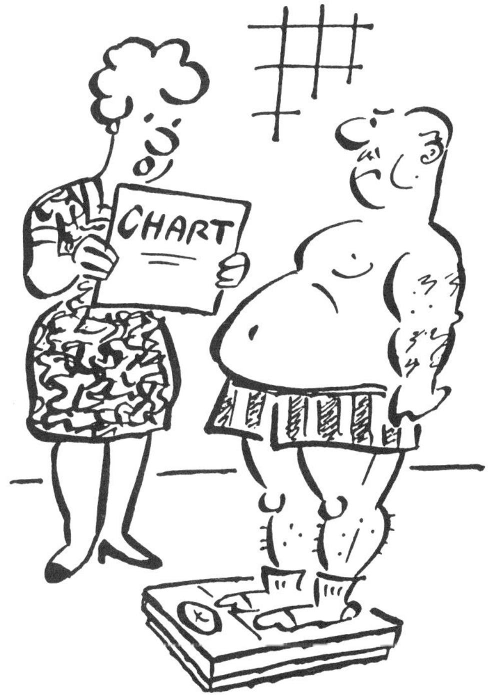

"According to your weight you should be 7' 6"."

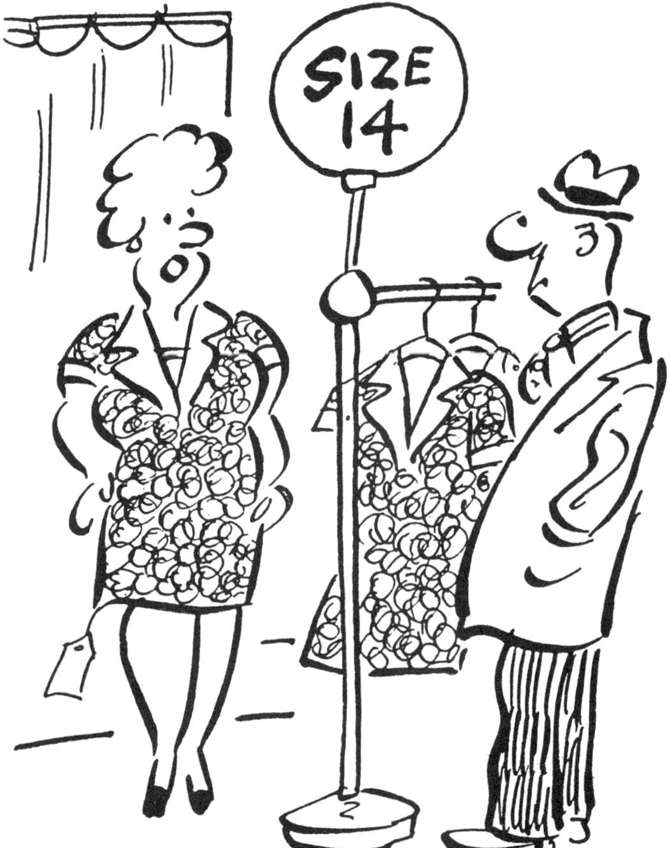

"It fits perfectly. I want to see if I can get it in a 12."

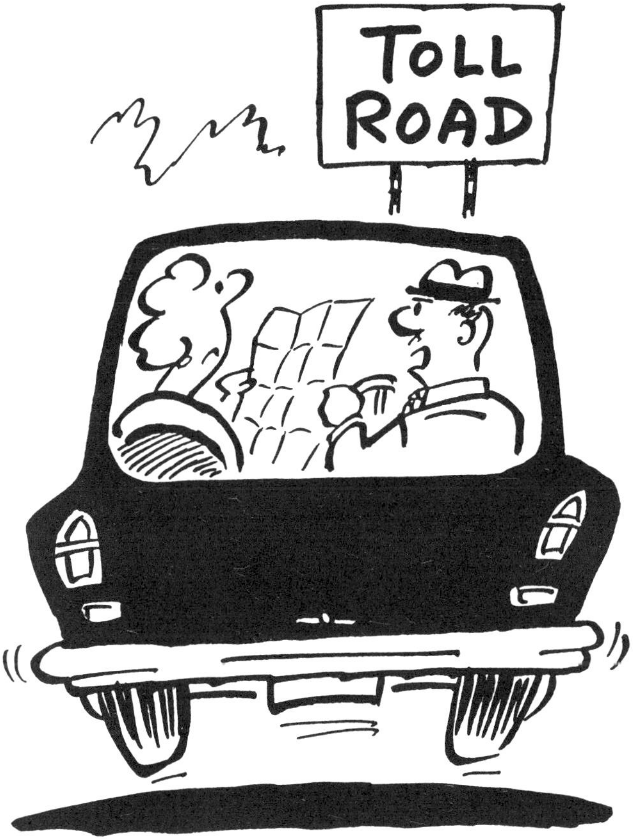

"Another brilliant piece of map reading!"

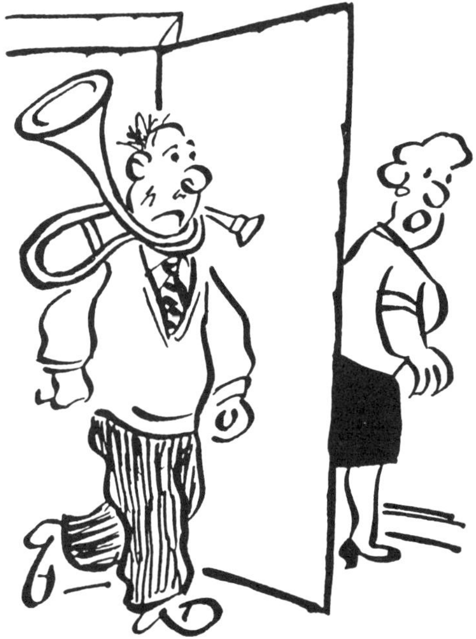

"He's stopped playing his trombone."

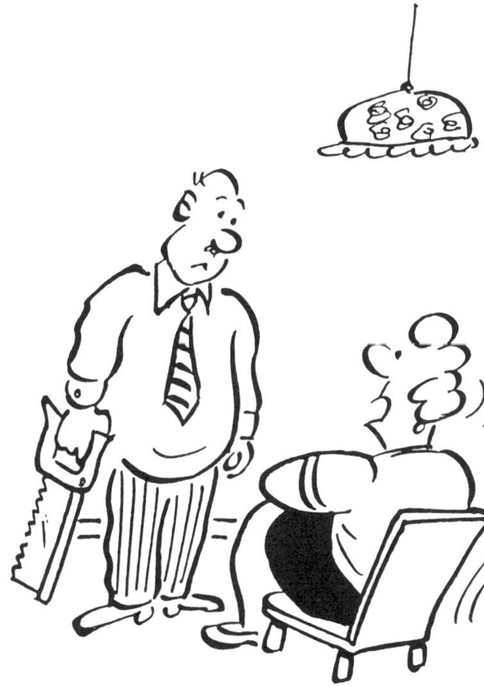

"It's still wobbling."

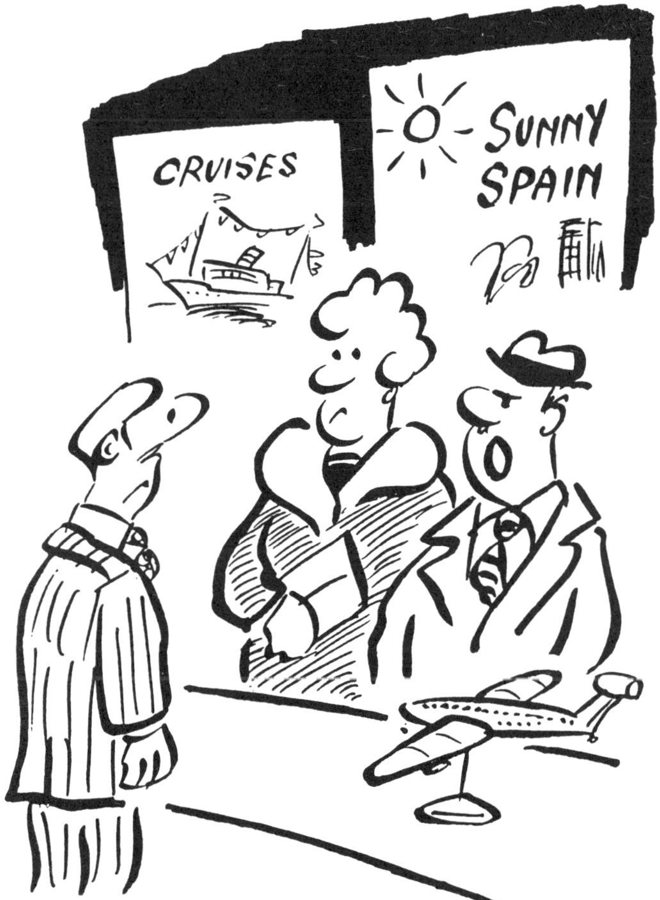

"Two round-the-world cruises on different ships."

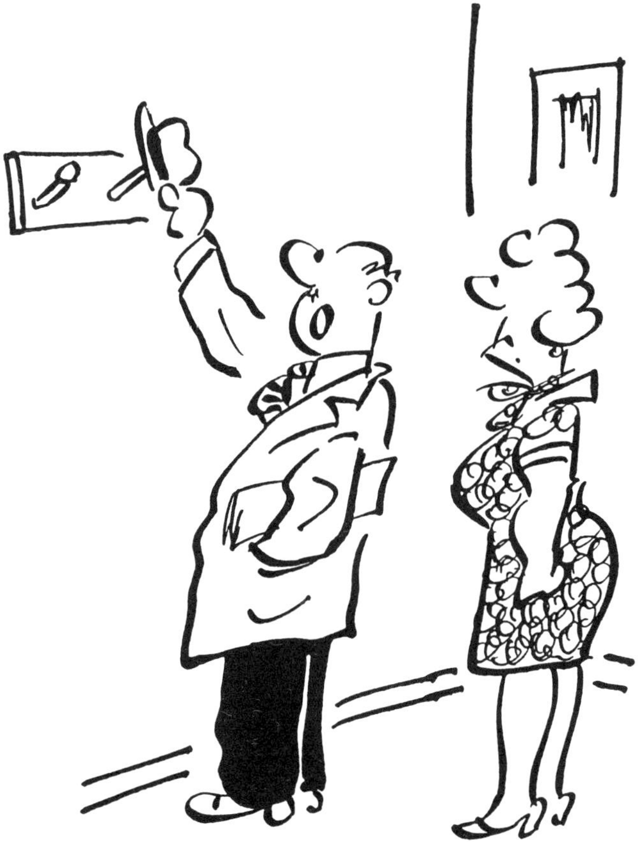

"I haggled with the boss and he finally agreed I'd get a 10% pay cut."

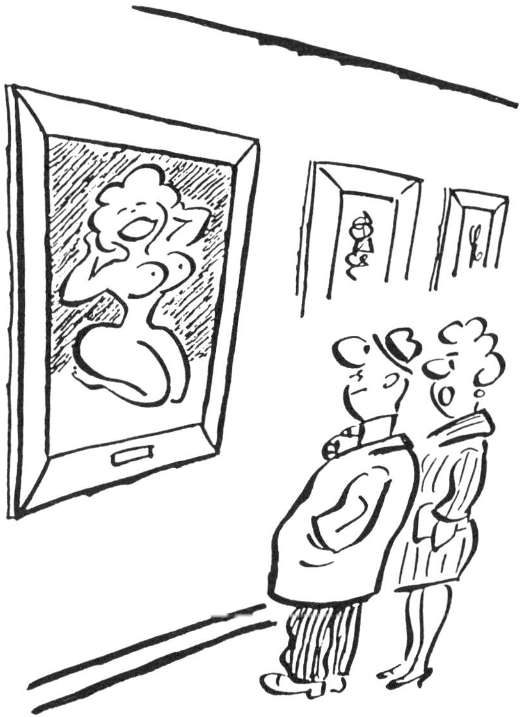

"Found one you understand?"

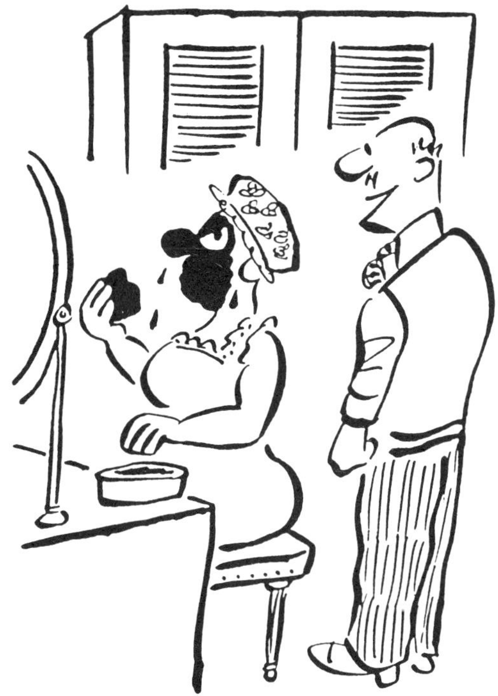

"My, I can see the improvement already!"

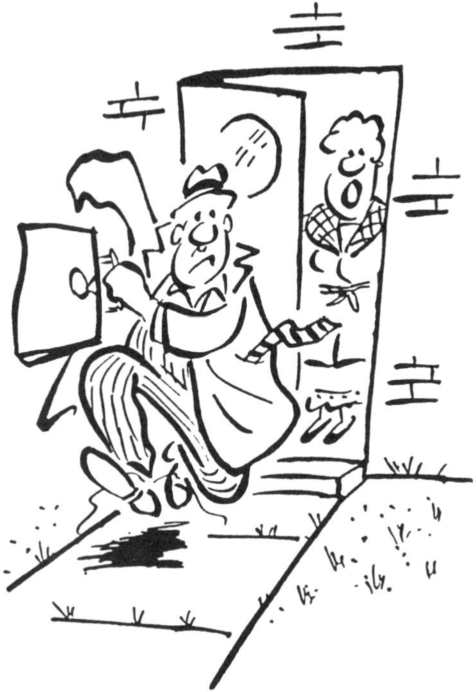

"Horace, today's Sunday!"

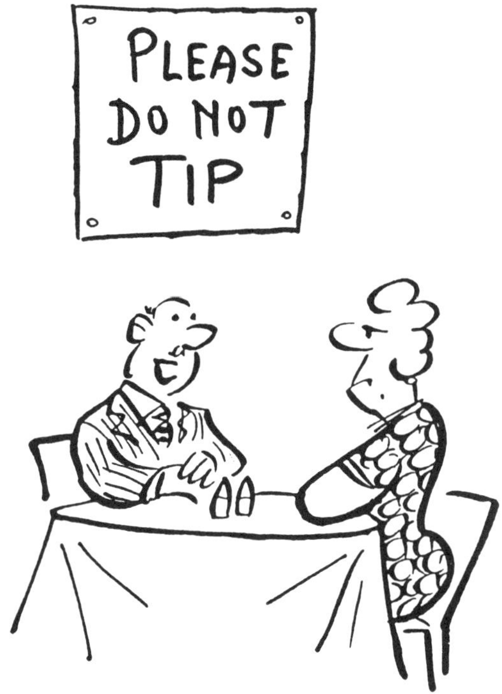

"I love this restaurant."

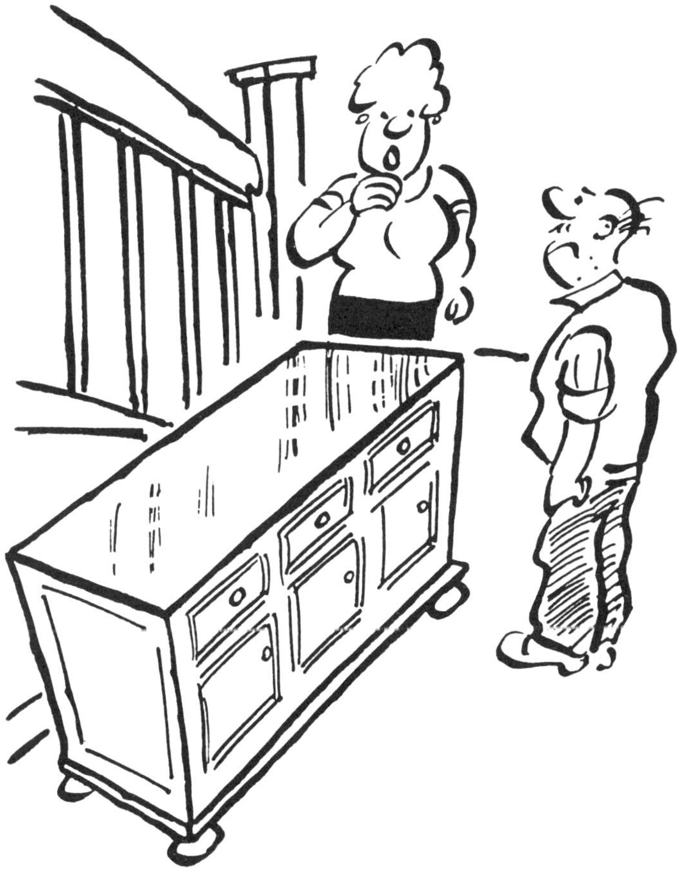

"On second thoughts I think I preferred it upstairs after all."

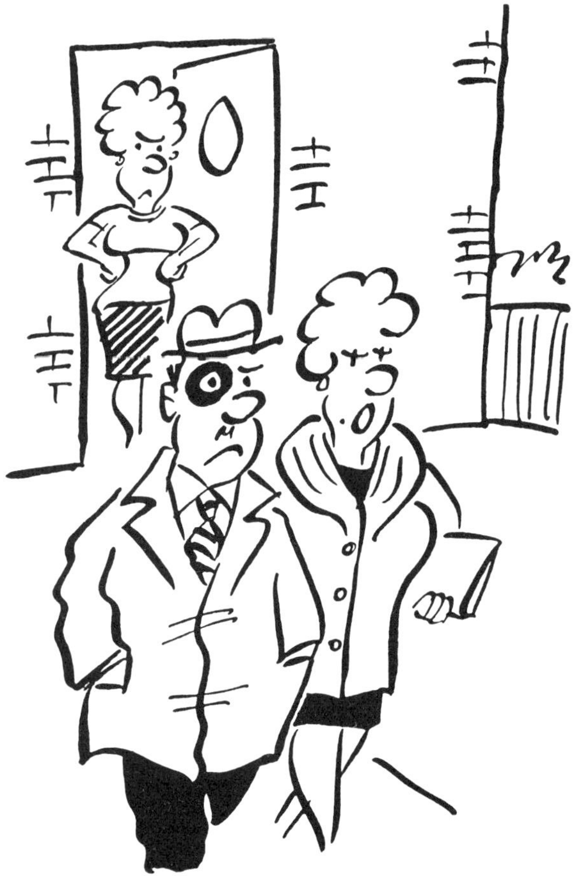

"I should have warned you. My friend Joan is very hot on womens' rights."

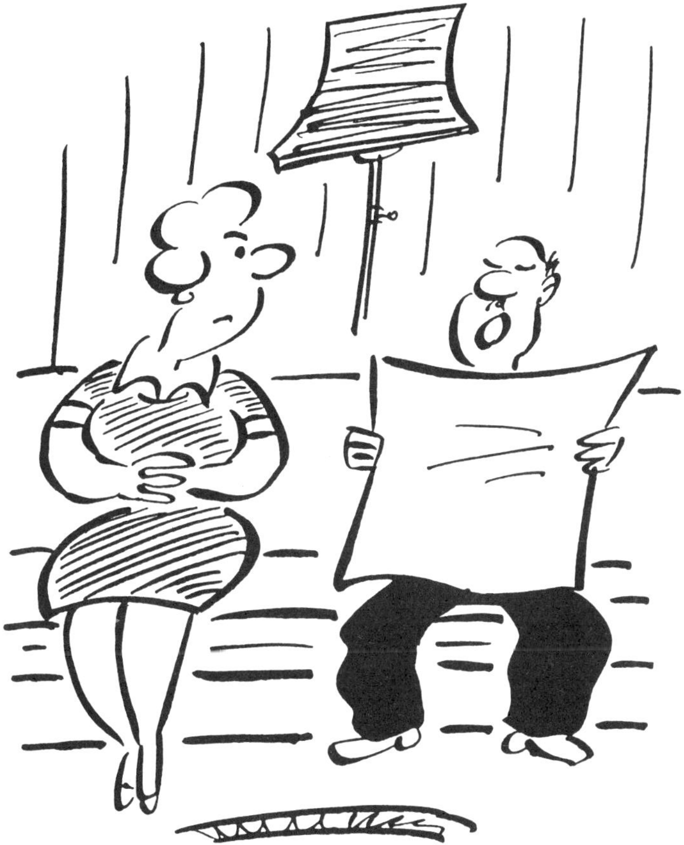

"Of course I wouldn't leave you for anyone else - once bitten twice shy."

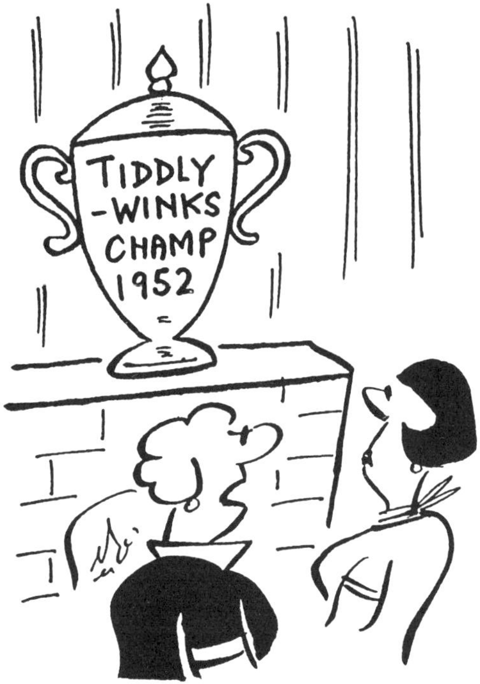

"Horace's star rose and fell very early."

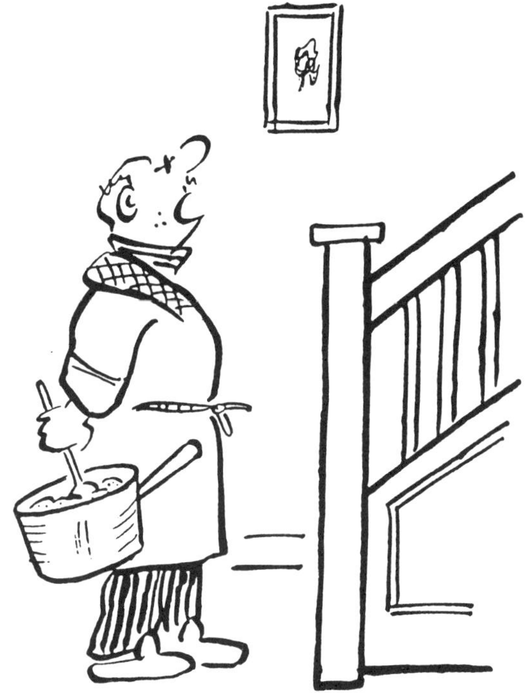

"Breakfast is ready. I've made some porridge!"

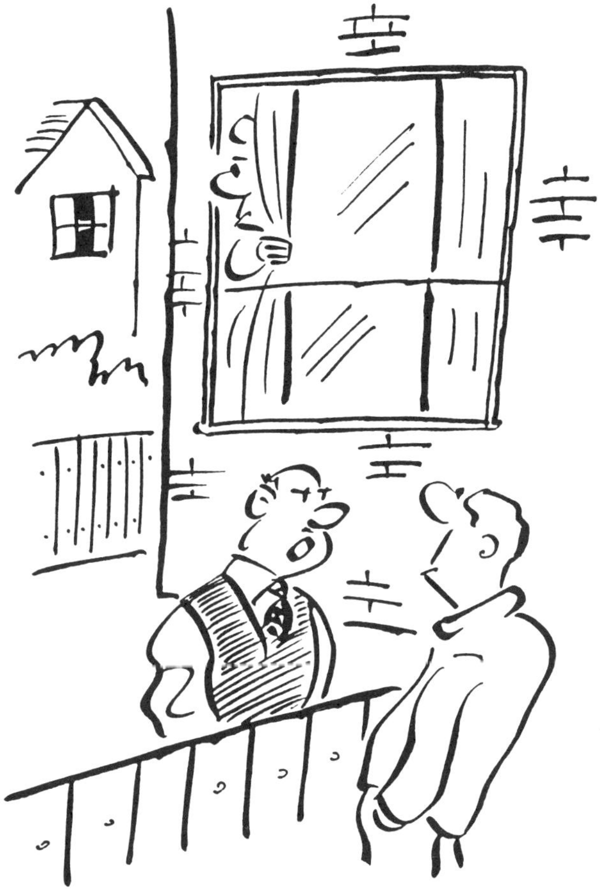

"Doris has been running her own neighbourhood watch scheme for years."

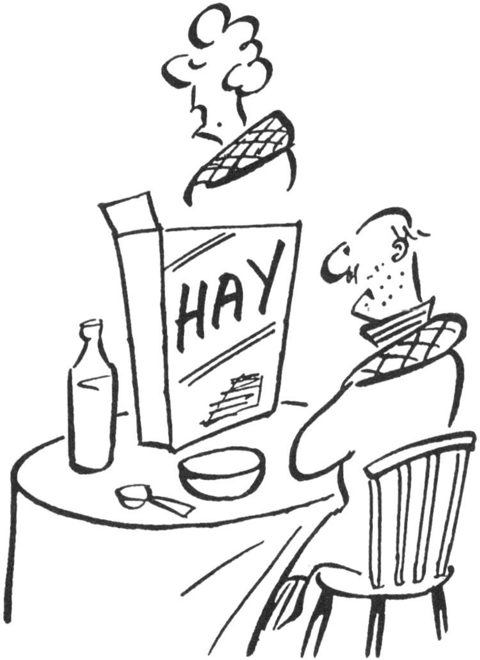

"It's a new high fibre cereal."

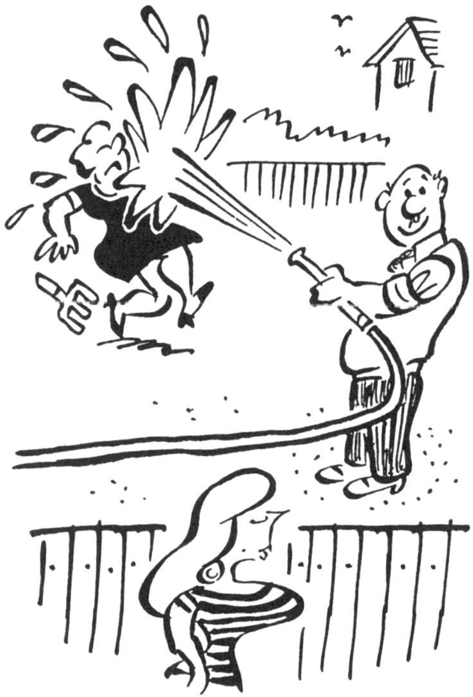

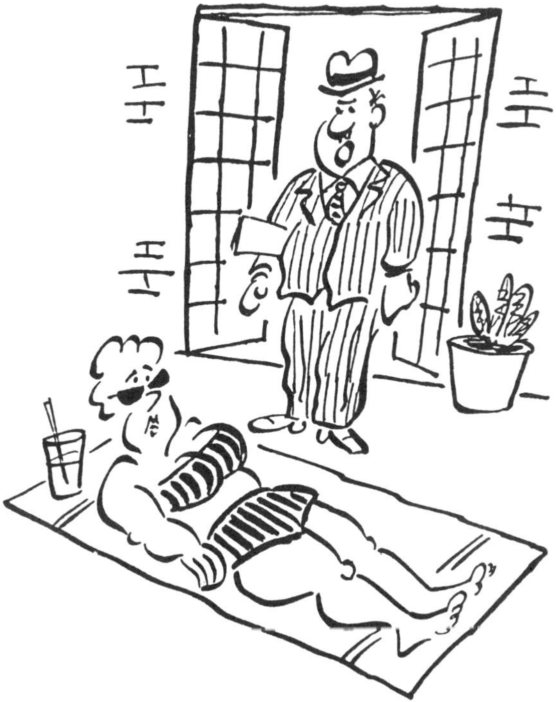

"Tea had better be ready!"

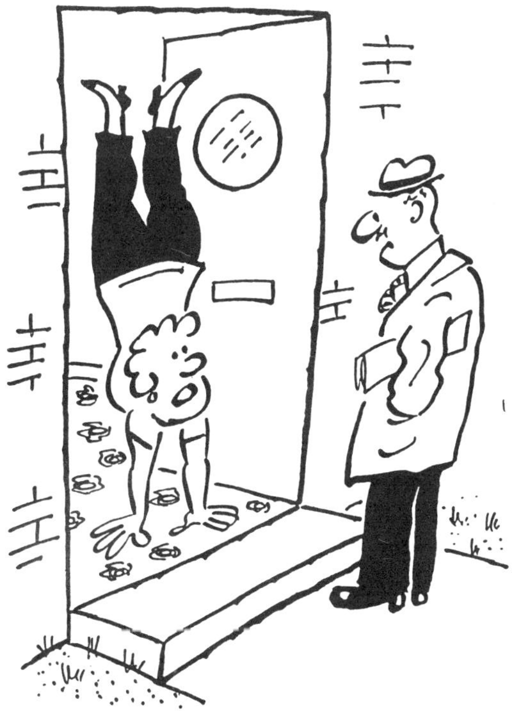

"Come in, the new carpet has arrived."

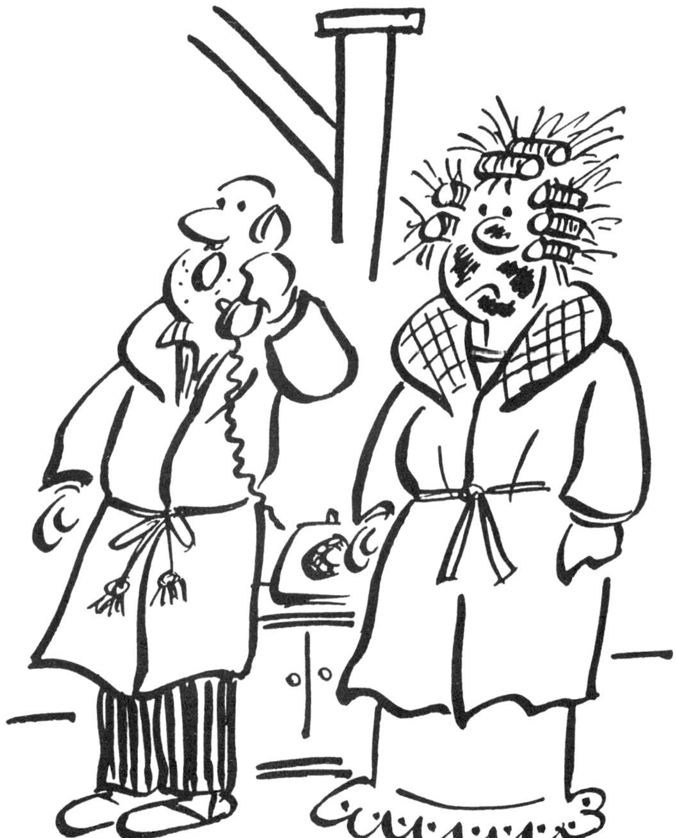

"The burglar ran off constable. I think my wife scared him."

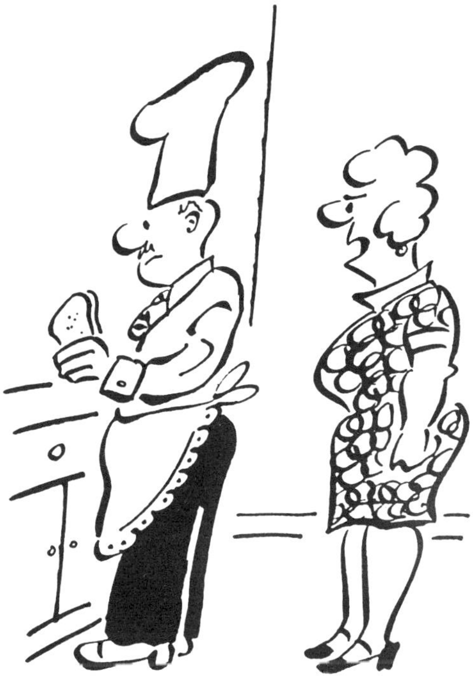

"Good heavens, Horace - You're only making toast!"

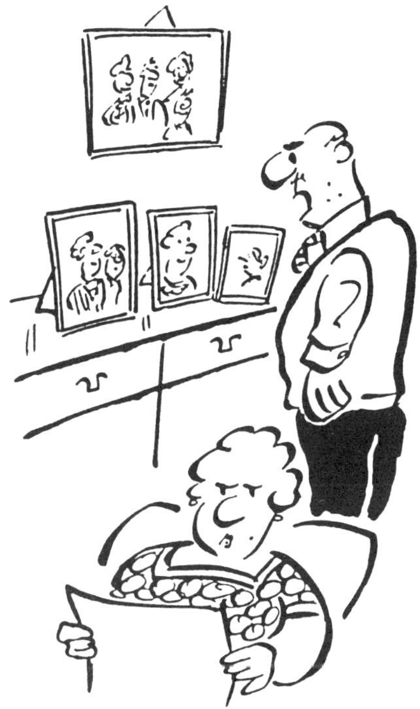

"I don't see **my** picture around here anywhere!"

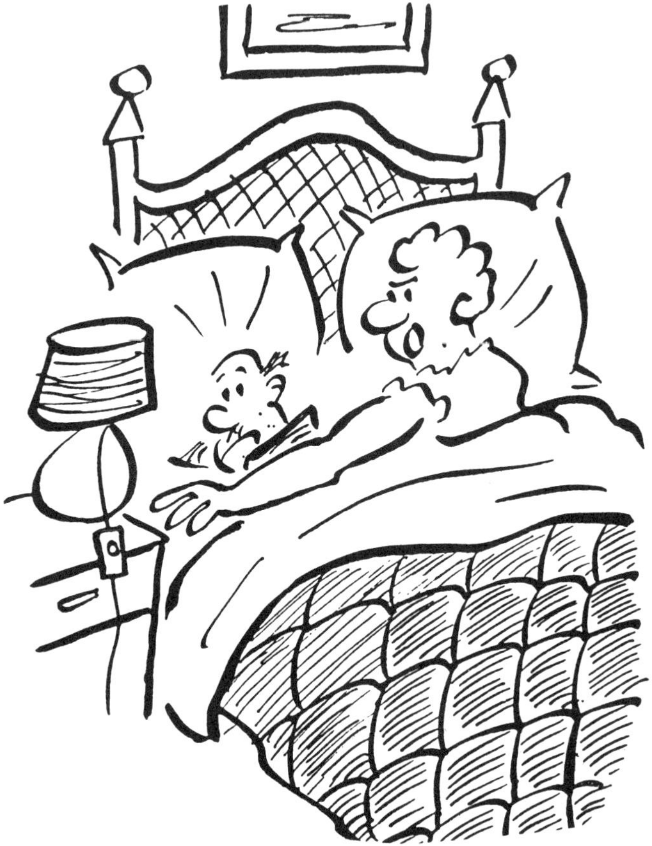

"Relax - I'm just leaning over to switch the light off."

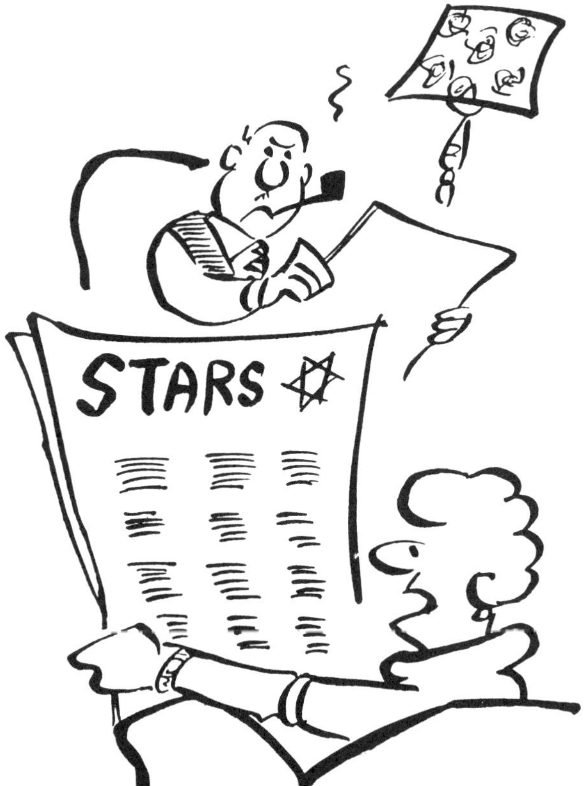

"According to your stars someone close to you deserves an expensive present."

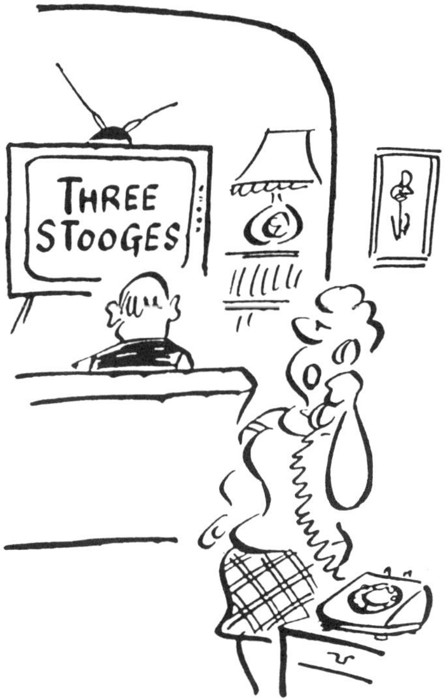

"The fourth stooge is watching the other three."

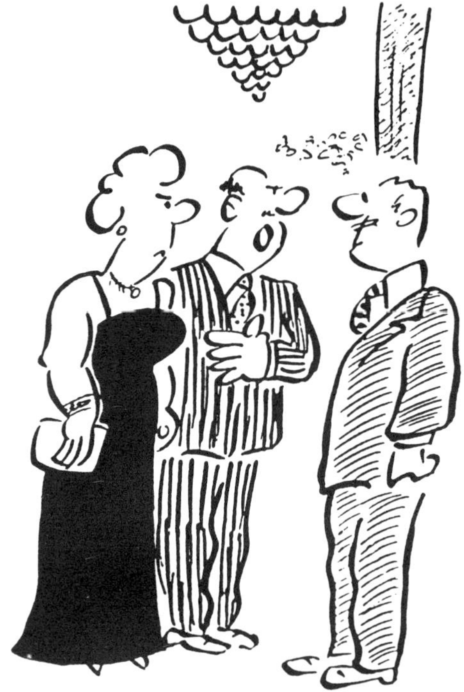

"This is Doris, my wife and most severest critic."

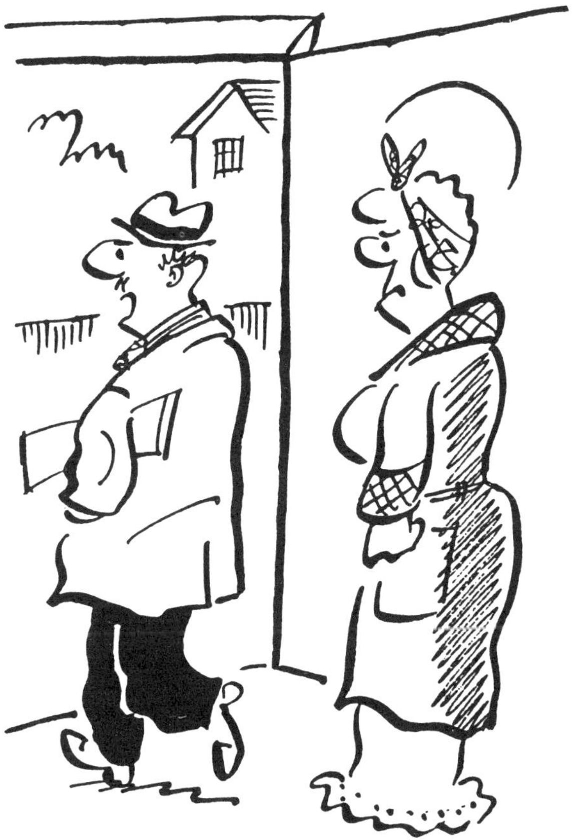

"If you want to buy me something for my birthday get me some industrial strength ear-plugs!"

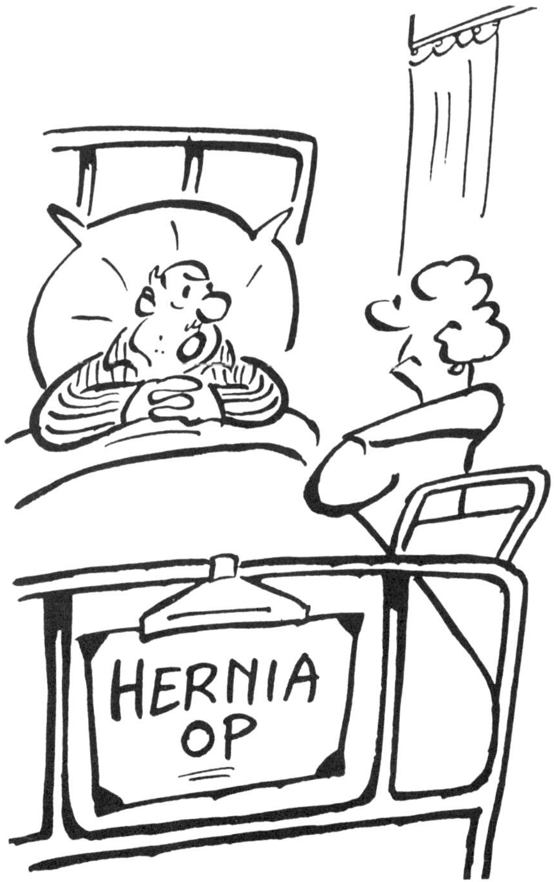

"Don't ever ask me to get one of your souffles out of the oven again!"

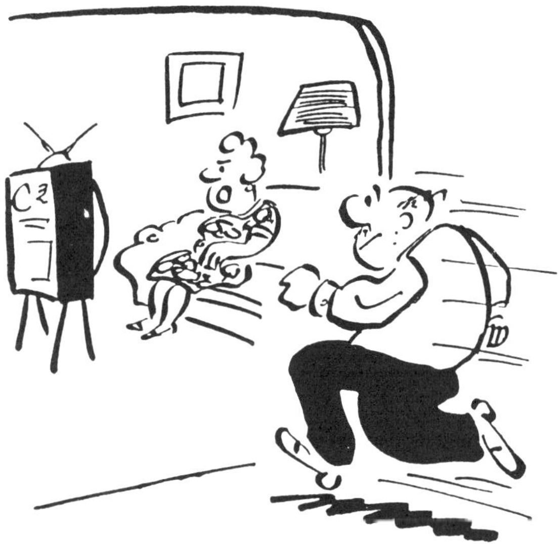

"Disgusting!"

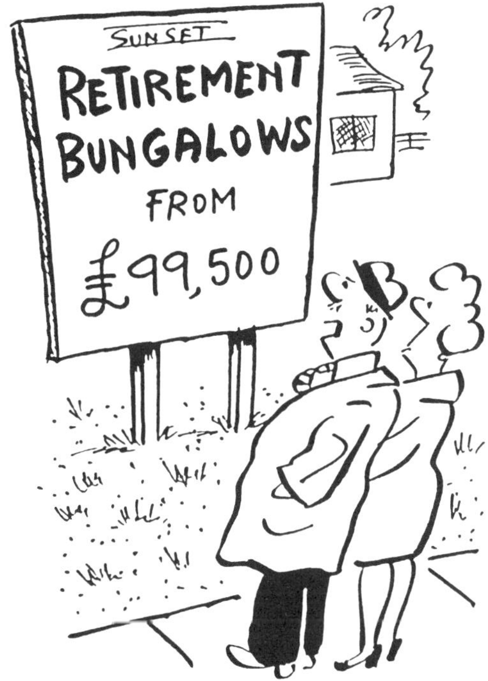

"It would mean us both getting jobs."

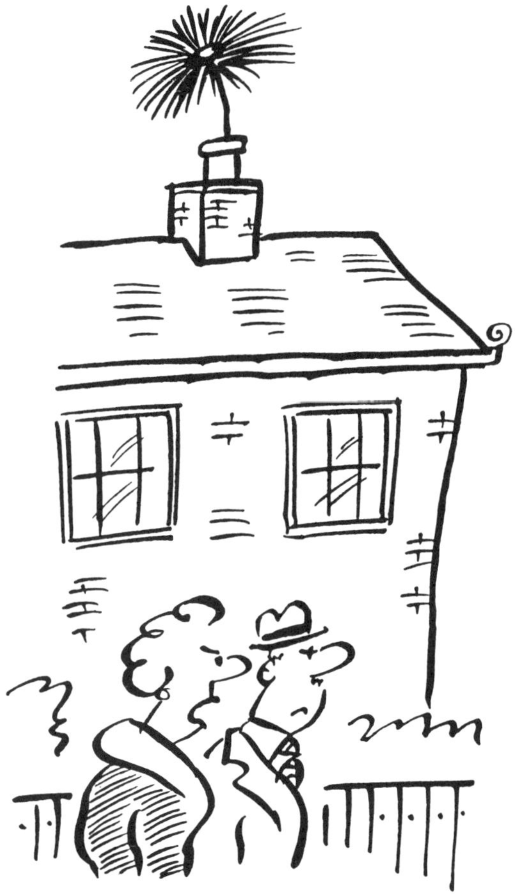

"Every other house has a satellite dish!"

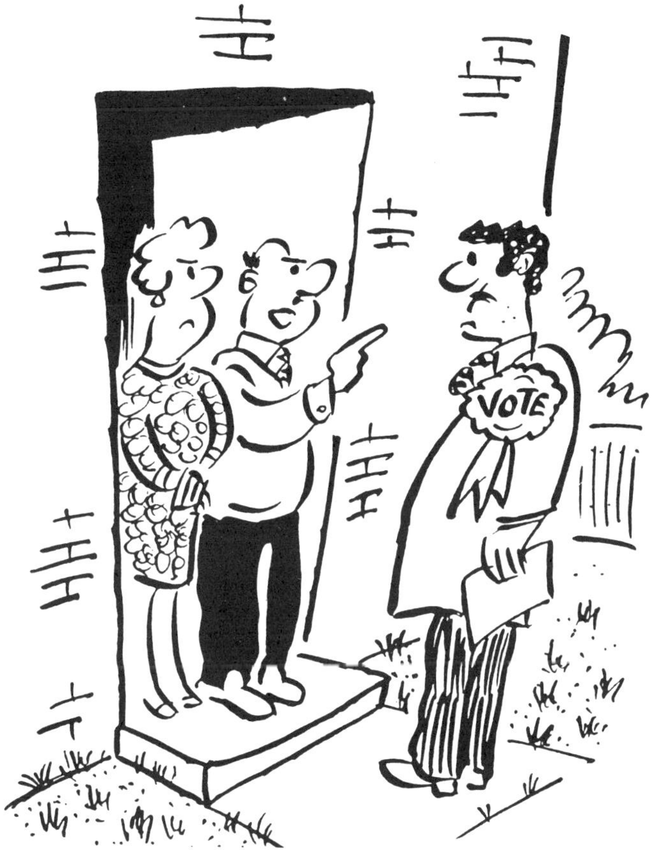

"I remember you, you drove us to the polling station once then made us walk back."

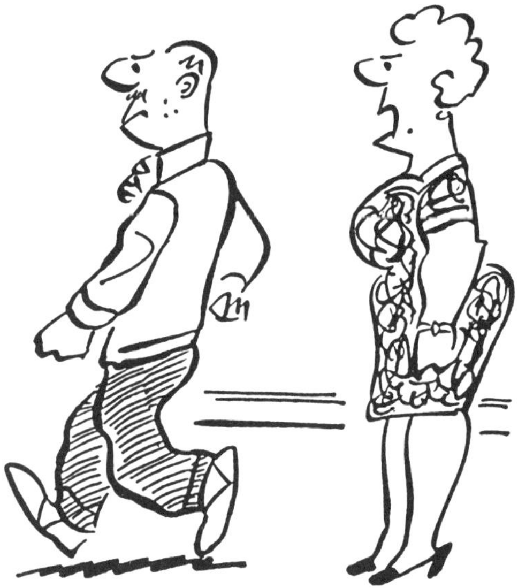

"Don't go - I haven't had the last word!"

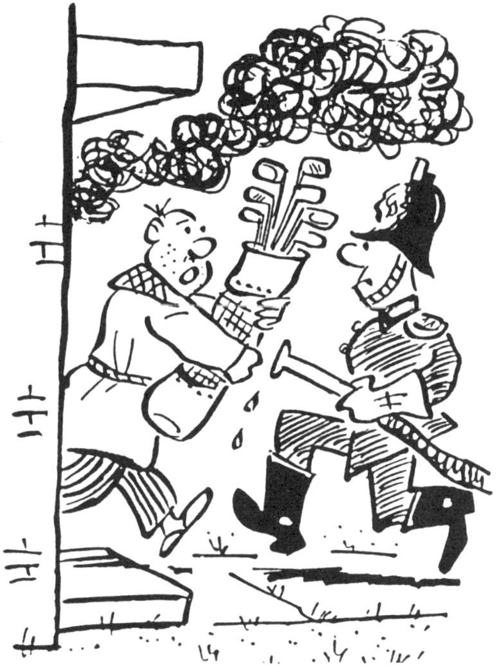

"Hurry - my wife is inside!"

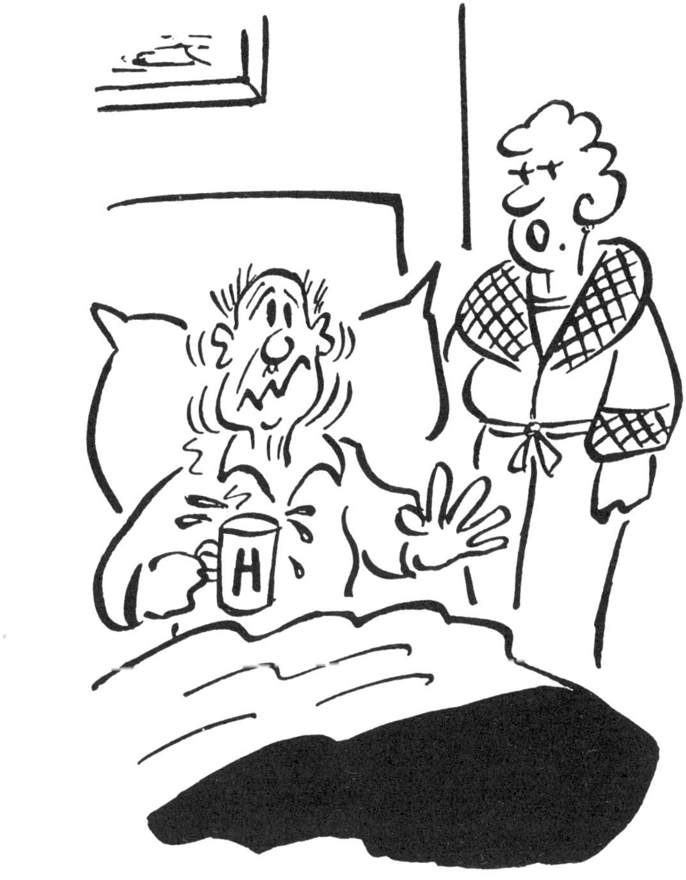

"Coffee without sugar - I thought I'd give you a jump start."

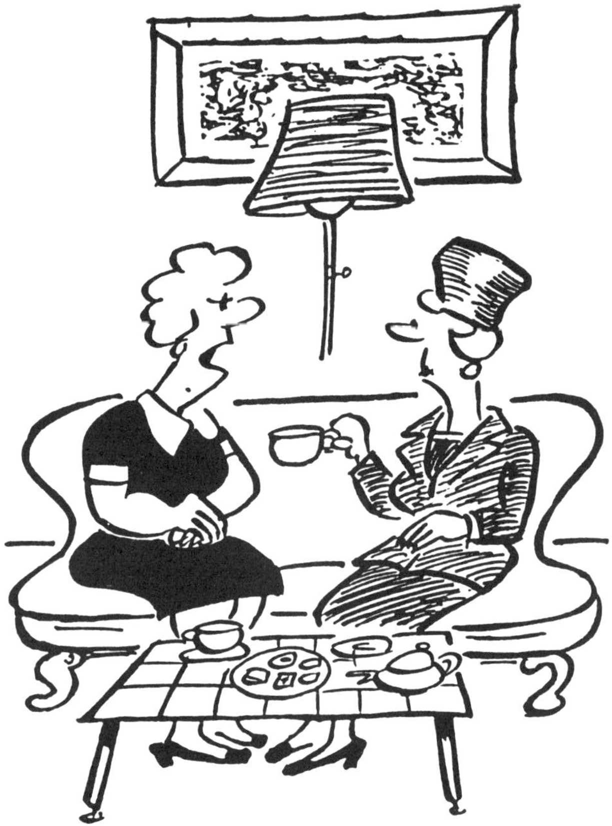

"But enough about my troubles . . .
how is ***your*** *husband?"*

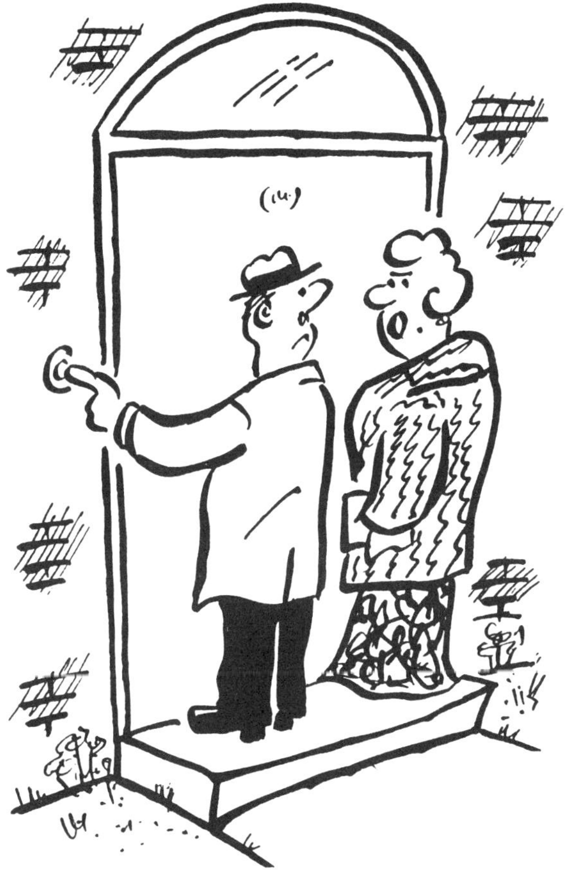

"They've got a video camera, so stay sober!"

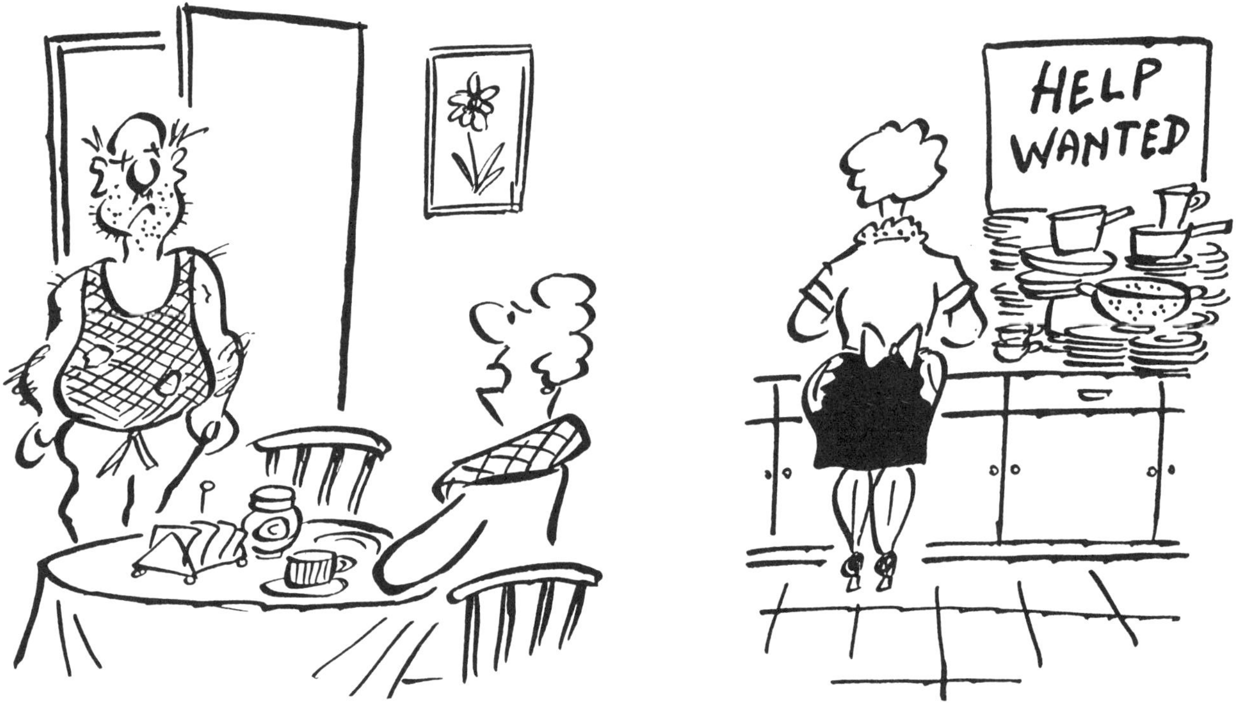

"Do I know you?"

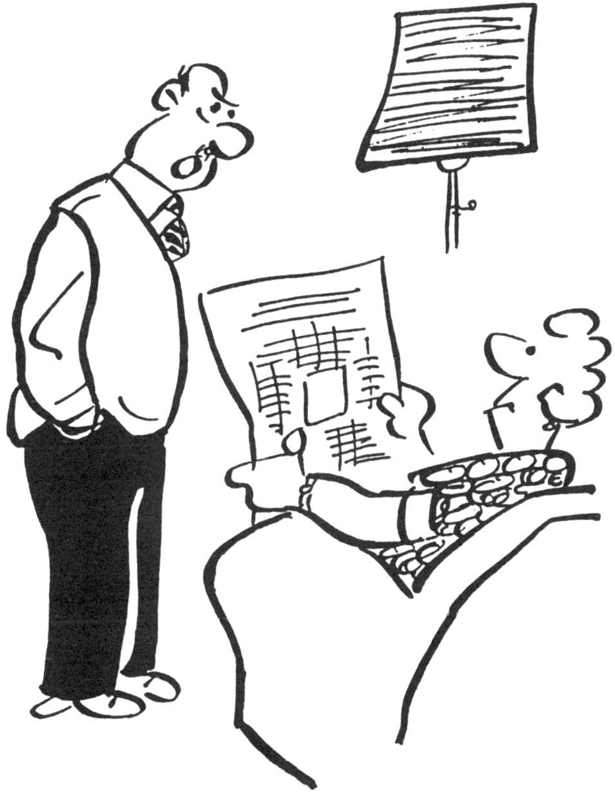

"What's the idea of calling me 'Nosey' in your diary?"

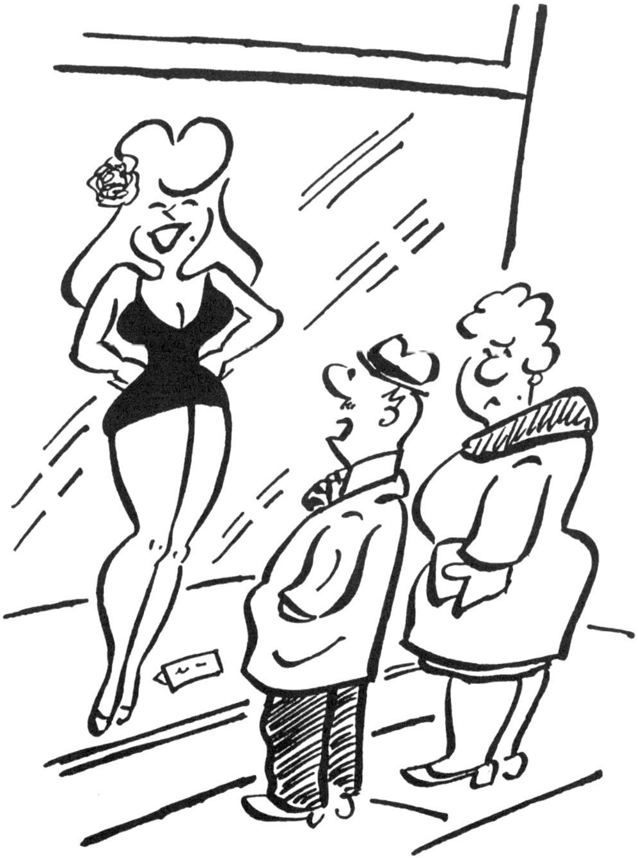

"So that's the bathing suit you want - do you think they do it in your shape?"

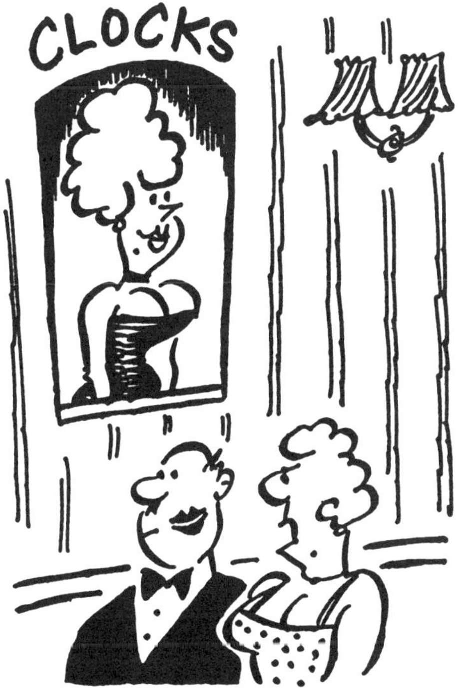

"How much did you tip her?"

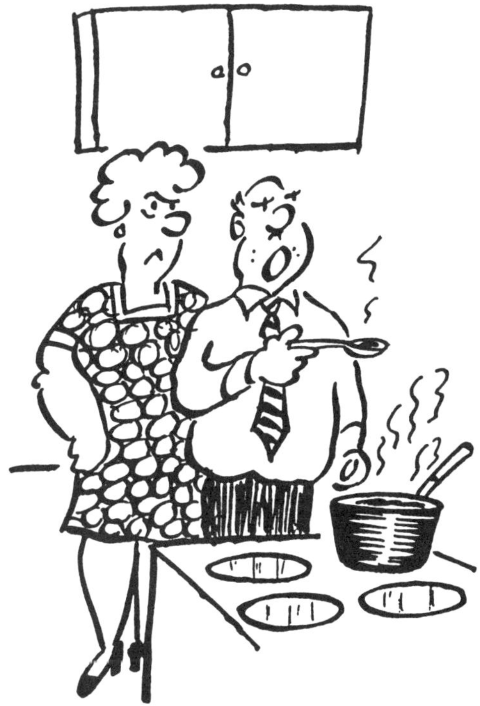

"It lacks something . . . I know - ***flavour.****"*

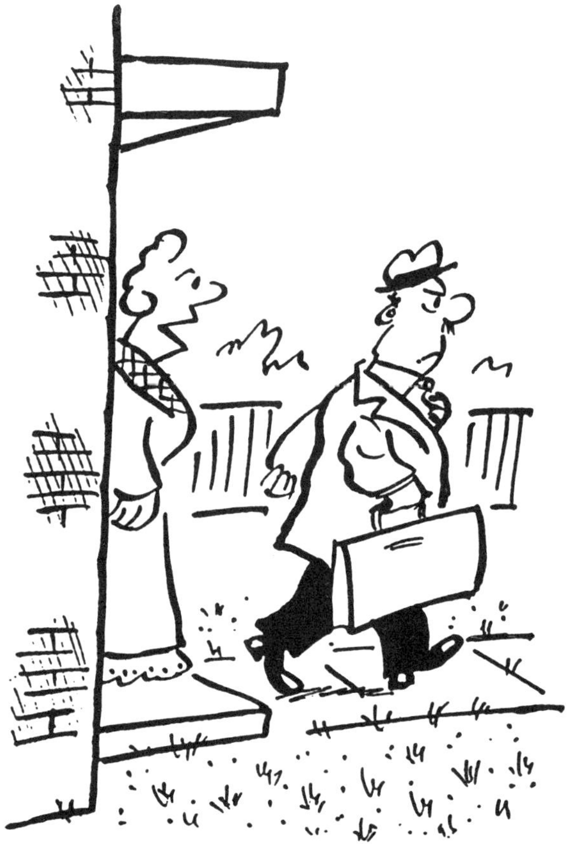

"Just remember Horace, it won't be a nice day unless you make it a nice day."

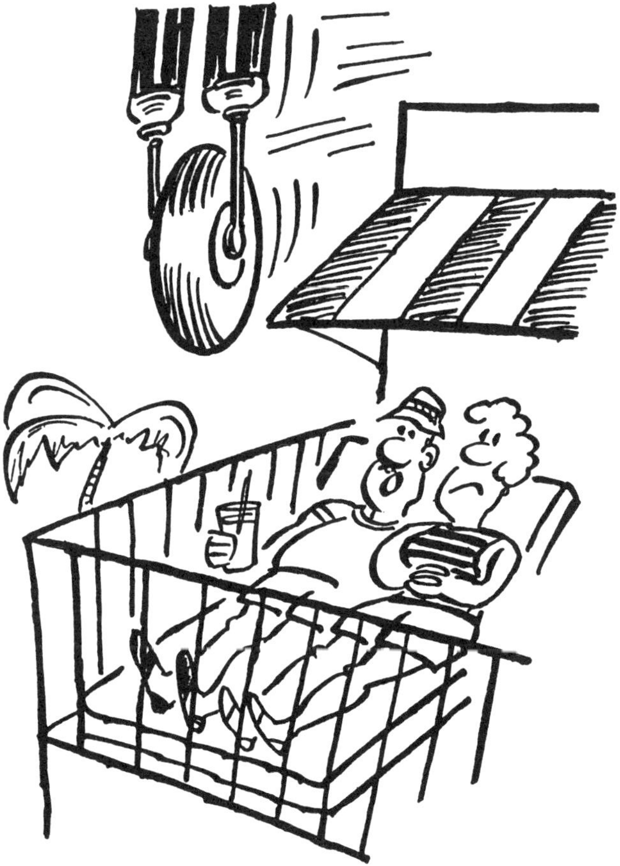

"The only thing the brochure got right was it being handy for the airport."

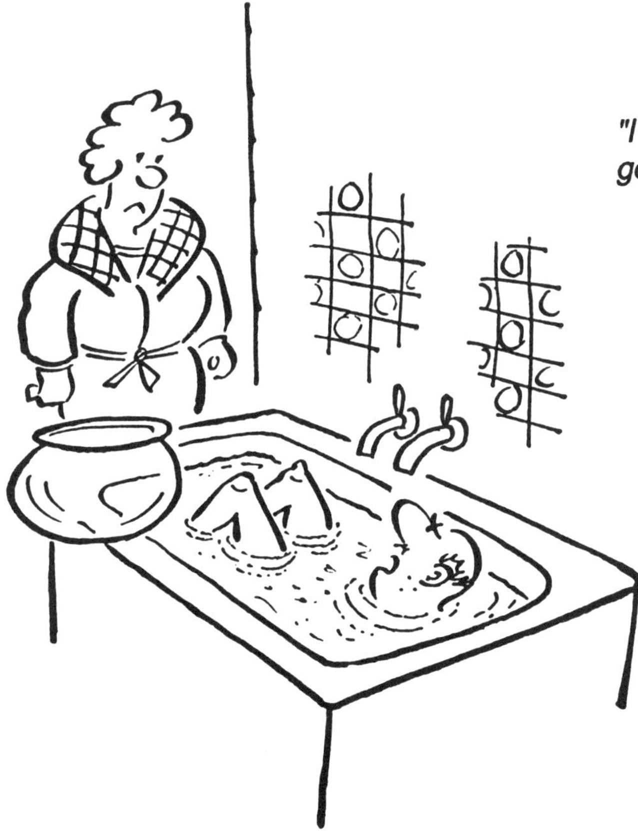

"I thought I'd give the goldfish a good swim."

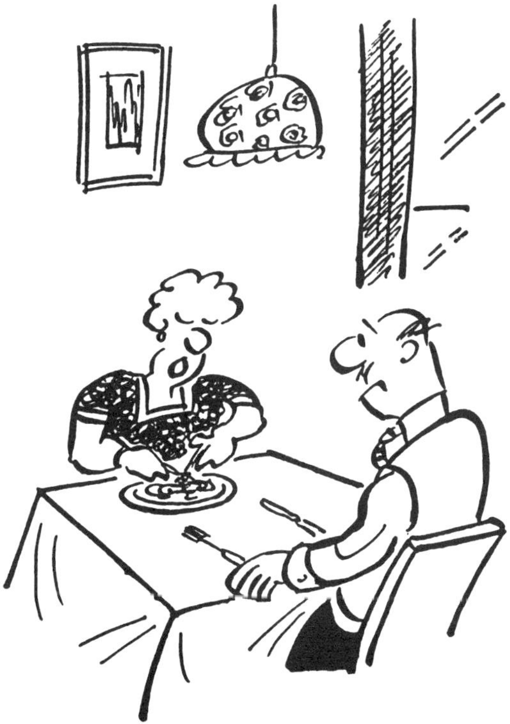

"The packet said 'serves one'."

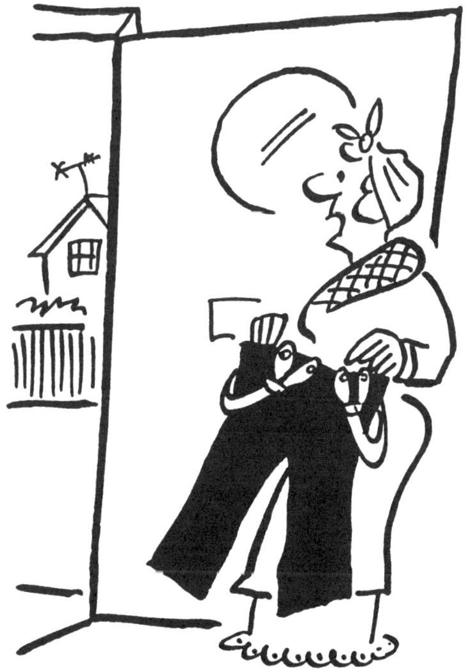

"I've been expecting you back."

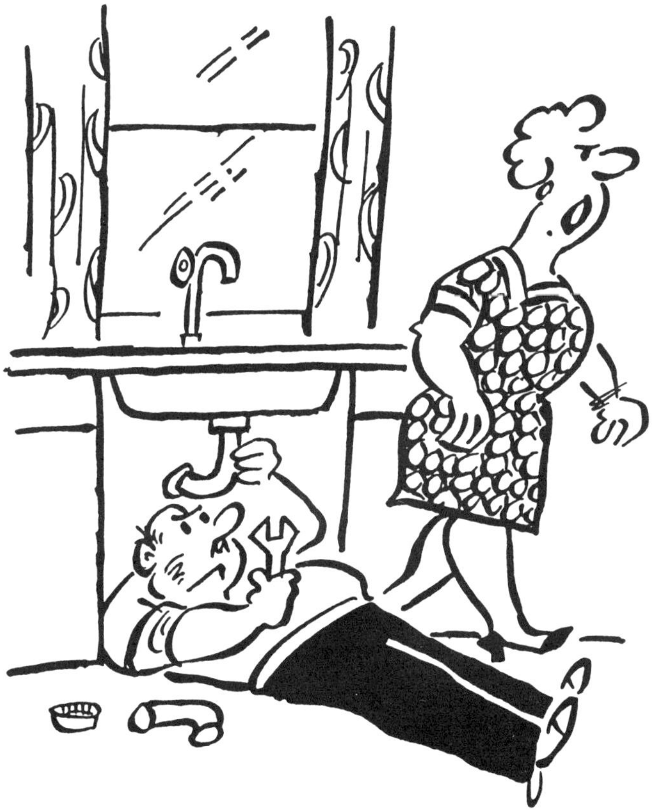

"While you're doing that, I'll go and call a plumber."

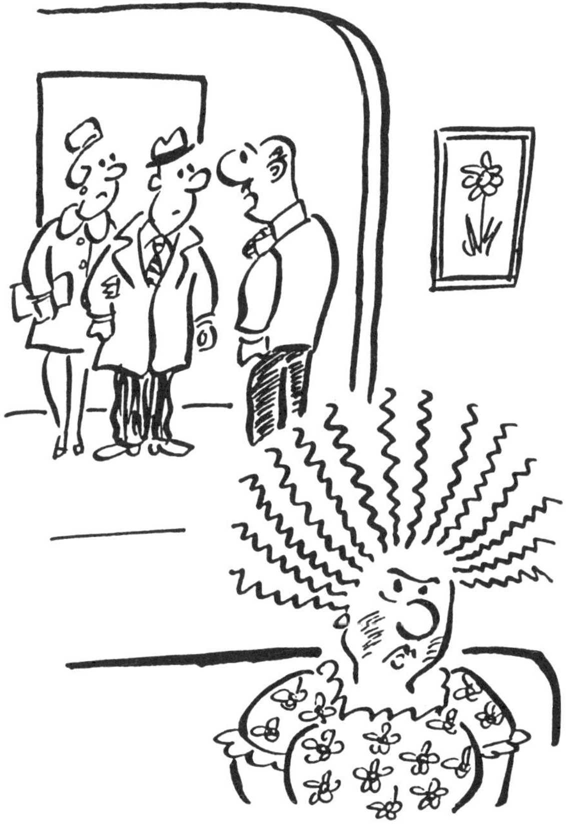

"Whatever you do don't mention her hair-do!"

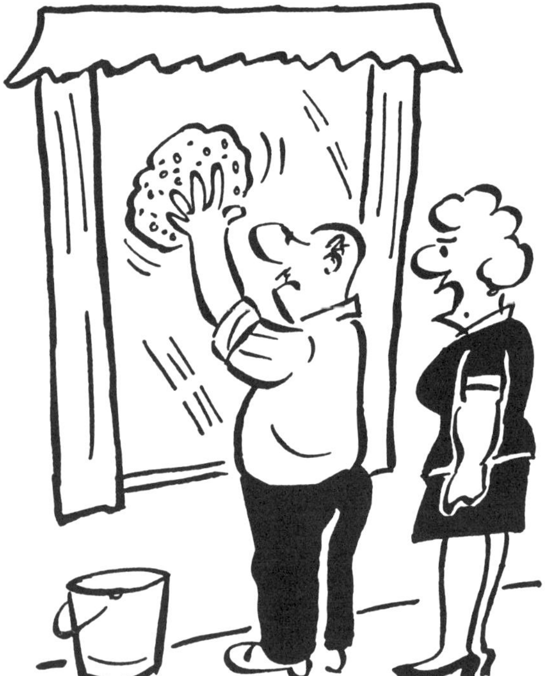

"What are you doing with my sponge cake?"

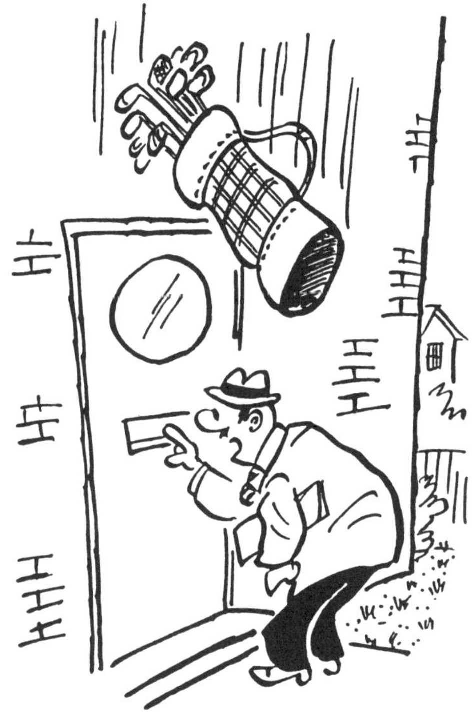

"Doris, are you still mad at me?"

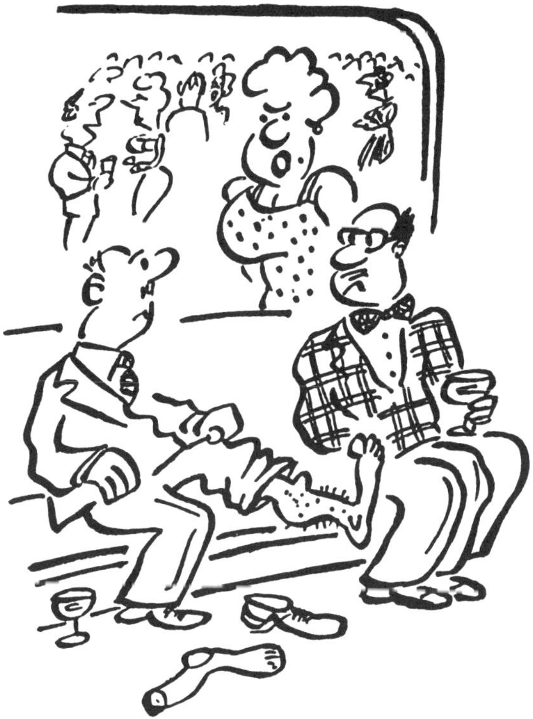

"Horace, Mr Plimsoll is a Doctor of Music!"

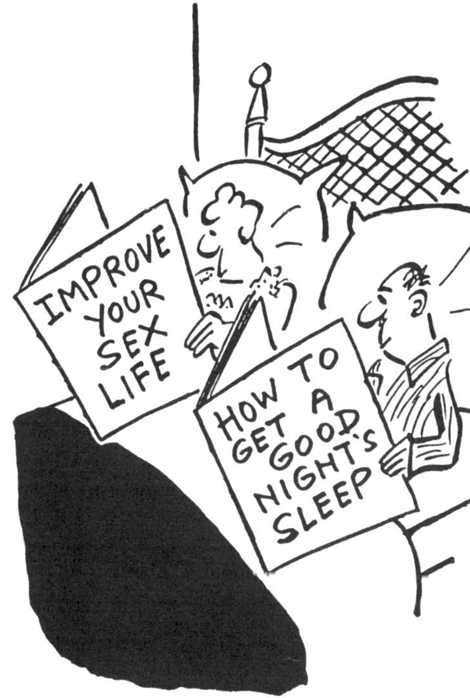

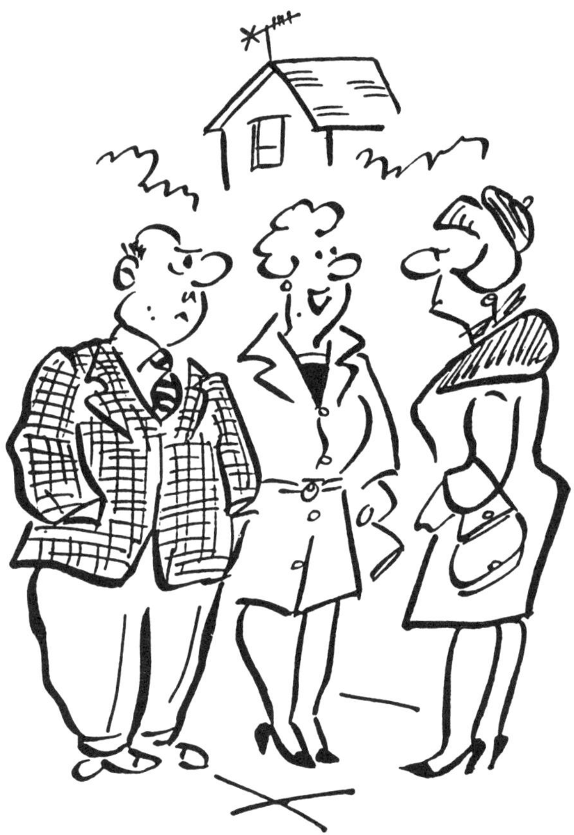

"Yes, this is the same chap I married in '56. It's just that he got fat and lost his hair."

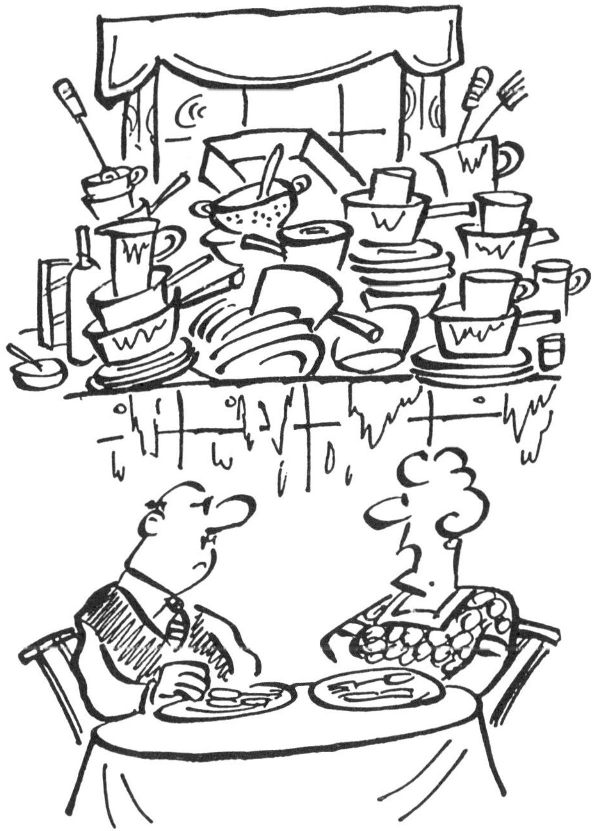

"Thanks, but don't ever prepare a meal again."

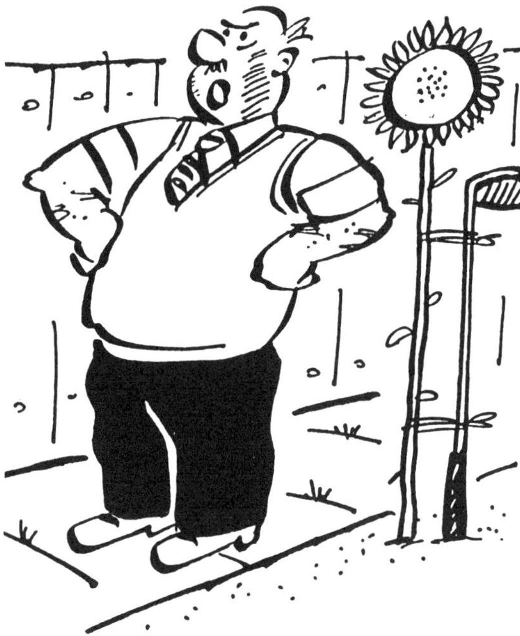

"DORIS!"

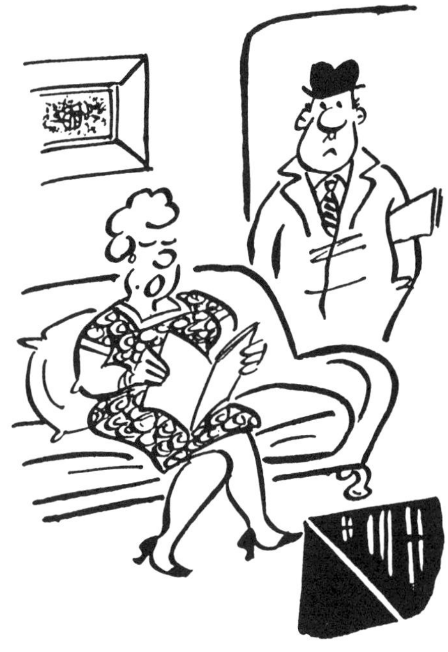

"Claire Rayner was talking about you today."

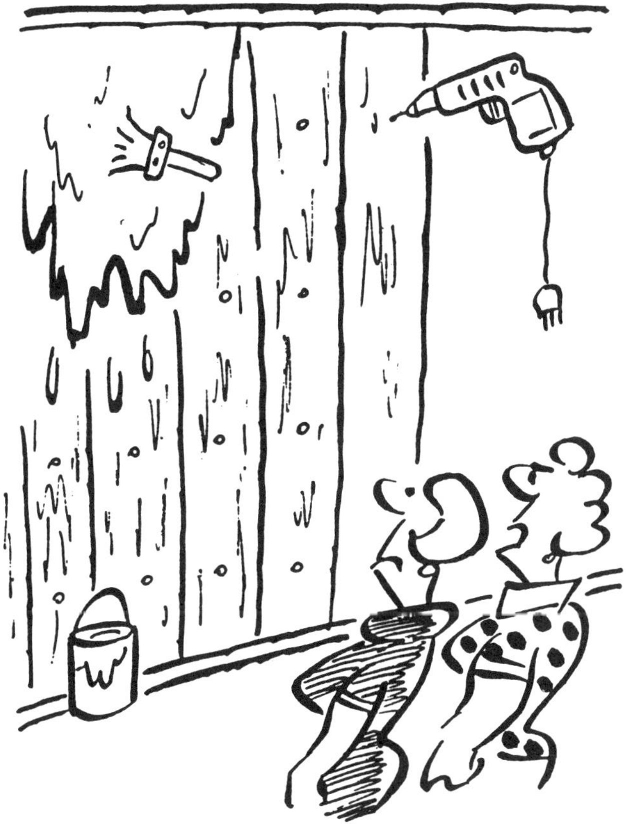

"That's the trouble, Horace never finishes anything."

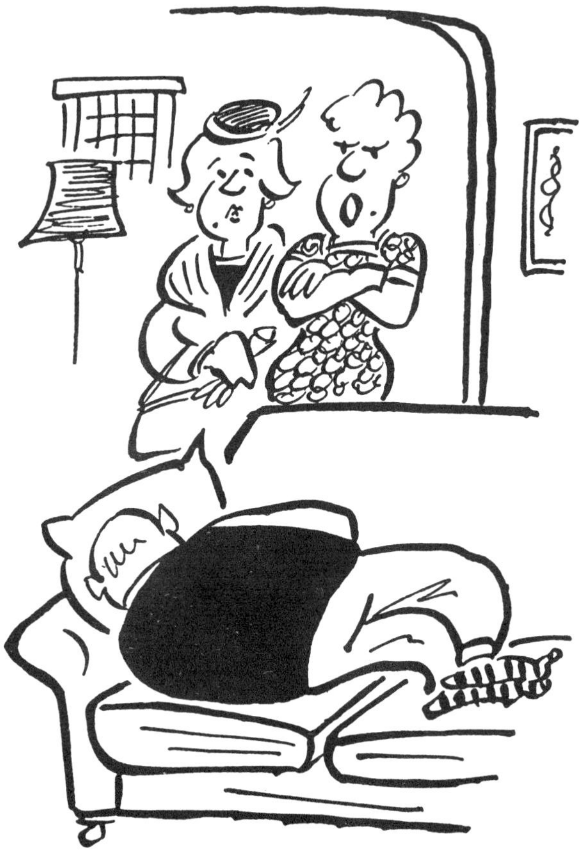

"If he did have a mid-life crisis, he probably slept through it."

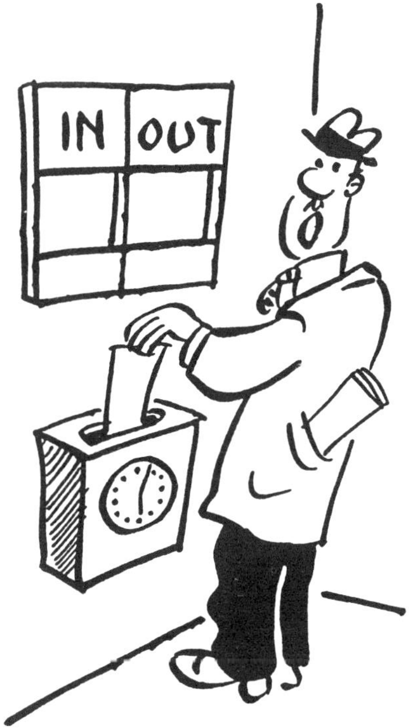

"Doris, I'm home!"

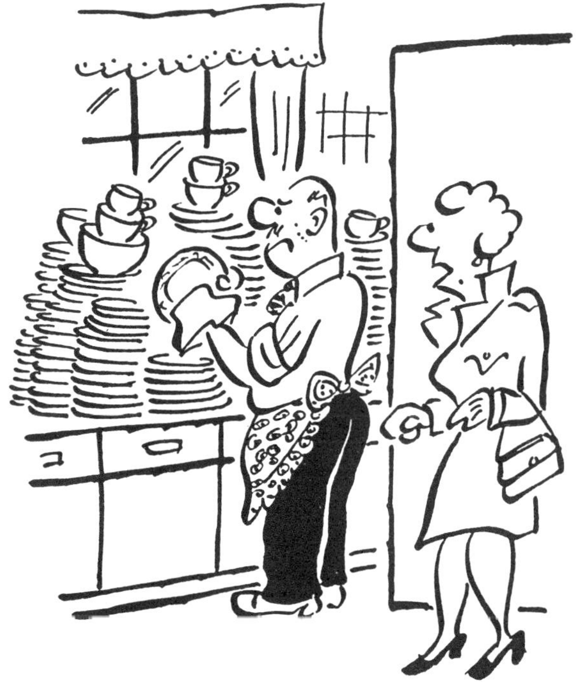

"I'm off to my pottery class."

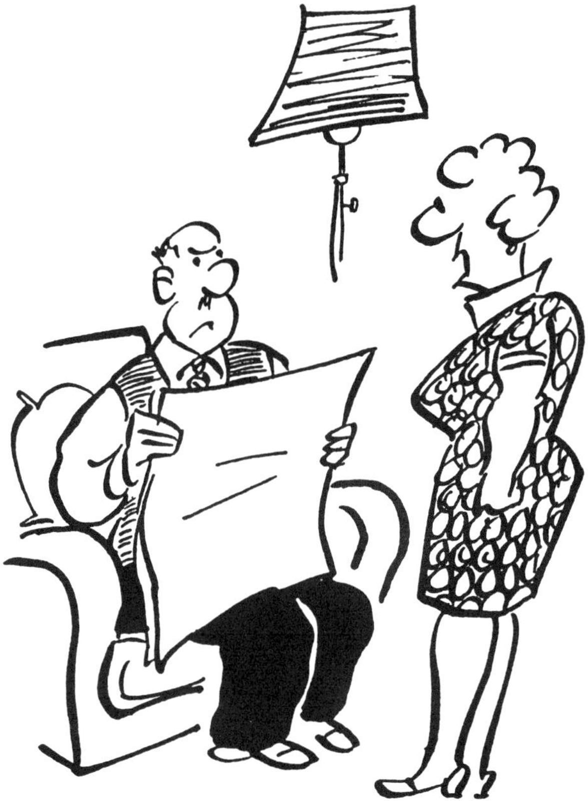

"I've just been looking at your face. Do you know you haven't got one laughter line?"

For original HORACE & DORIS cartoons
Please telephone: (021) 4295861